Junior Soccer –
A Manual for Coaches

Bischops/Gerards

Junior Soccer
A Manual for Coaches

Meyer & Meyer Sport

Orginal title: Handbuch für Kinder- und Jugendfußball
© 1997 by Meyer & Meyer Verlag, Aachen/Germany
Translated by Robert McMurray

British Library Cataloguing in Publication Data
A catalogue record for this book is available from the British Library

Bischops, Klaus:
Junior Soccer: A Manual for Coaches/ Klaus Bischops ; Heinz-Willi Gerards.
2nd. Ed. - Oxford : Meyer & Meyer Sport (UK) Ltd., 2003
ISBN 1-84126-000-2

All rights reserved. Except for use in a review, no part of this publication may be reproduced, stored in
a retrieval system, or transmitted, in any form or by any means now known or hereafter invented
without the prior written permission of the publisher. This book may not be lent, resold, hired out or
otherwise disposed of by way of trade in any form, binding or cover other than that which is published,
without the prior written consent of the publisher.

© 1999 by Meyer & Meyer Sport (UK) Ltd
2nd Edition 2003
Adelaide, Auckland, Budapest, Graz, Johannesburg, Miami,
Olten (CH), Oxford, Singapore, Toronto
Member of the World
Sport Publishers' Association (WSPA)

e-mail: verlag@m-m-sports.com
Cover design: Walter Neumann N&N Design Studio, Aachen
Cover Photo: Sportpressefoto Bongarts, Hamburg
Photos inside: Michael von Fisenne, Fotoagentur, Aachen; Dr. Klaus Bischops
Drawings: Susanne Dalley, Aachen
Printed and bound by
FINIDR s. r. o., Český Těšín
ISBN 1-84126-000-2

Table of Contents

1 Foreword to "Junior Soccer: A Manual for Coaches" by Berti Vogts, Former Official Coach of the German National Soccer Team

Dear Sportsfans,

The supporting of top achievement in sport, the fulfillment of educational functions, the imparting of a sense of community and joy of living are all demands made on coaches of, or those responsible for, junior soccer teams. Through the publication of this book the DJK (German Youth Clubs) is demonstrating that these demands are not only theoretical but should also be put into practice. Its contents will be a guide for the daily work with adolescents.

Anybody active in the field of youth work has a lot responsibility for the future. It will depend on the involvement of the clubs and the qualifications of all those involved as to whether junior soccer can show a growth in numbers again.

I trained children and teenagers for many years and know not only what it means to bear the responsibility and the educational commitment that work with adolescents requires, but also the pleasure that one experiences again and again that such work brings. "Soccer is fun" should not just be the motto of a soccer recruiting competition started by the German Soccer Federation but also the motto for their involvement in junior soccer.

If coaches and others responsible succeed in communicating this fun in the area between play and competition, then I can look to the future of junior soccer with confidence.

Berti Vogts

2   Introduction

The work in the area of sport for children and adolescents is one of the most important challenges for any sports club. For this reason training must bear in mind the physical and psychological development of the players. To be able to achieve this goal, there is a special need for properly trained coaches, practice-coaches and others responsible in the youth sections of sports clubs.

This is why the introducing of adolescents to the game of soccer and further training should be of the highest quality. In this book, therefore, we want to try to assist and support all those involved in sports training for children and adolescents. Basic suggestions and information are set out in a concise and easy-to-understand way, but will need to be adjusted to individual playing field conditions.

Our book, with its more than 100 training units, is directed at the „on-the-spot" practician who, after finishing work, devotes himself to his hobby as „football-mediator". From the Midgets to the Juniors-A's, tips on warming-up, areas of the game to be concentrated on and winding down can be found in every unit.

The introduction provides coaches, practice-coaches and teachers with information on the importance of coaching children and adolescents. An appendix contains interesting tips on questions of organisation, team spirit and social activities.

The book originated out of daily practice with the large junior section of a soccer team and for this reason its contents can be applied directly by those involved in working with adolescents. Each training unit begins by setting out the goal to be achieved, goes on to sports activities and finishes with tips for the coach.
   We both wish those responsible in junior soccer success and fun in their work.

Heinz-Willi Gerards
Klaus Bischops

3 Soccer Training for Children and Adolescents

The Importance of Sports Training for Children and Adolescents

Training of children and teenagers is defined by certain emphases. In terms of compre-hensiveness and intensity it is not a scaled-down version of training for seniors by any means. Children and adolescents must be trained in a way that corresponds to the particular stages of their individual development. In this context the following points must be made:
- Training with children is chiefly designed to retain and reinforce enjoyment and pleasure of playing soccer.
- With teenagers each training session pursues the improvement of skills (techniques, understanding of the game, willingness to take risks etc), but more than that, the individual enjoyment of the game must be maintained through constantly varied training.
- Coaching in a form appropriate for children and adolescents requires a coach familiar with the developmental stages of adolescents and tailors the coaching accordingly (developmental psychology).
- Children learn first and foremost by demonstration and imitation (imitative learning). For this reason everyone involved in coaching adolescents should be capable of demonstrating both the technical and the more non-competitive aspects of the game.
- In order to achieve training goals as effectively as possible, a Junior Coach requires a certain ability to impart knowledge (personal subject knowledge).
- Working with children and adolescents – and this goes for soccer as well – always involves an educational function. In his or her capacity as teacher, the coach automatically becomes a role-model. This must be borne in mind in all decisions and actions.
- Educational goals in the context of the game might be: independence, developing a sense of responsibility, learning to get on with others, accepting the decisions of others, developing team spirit, being able to fit in, accepting criticism, learning fair play etc.
- The creation of an open and cheerful training atmosphere is a positive prerequirement for motivational training sessions but also for involvement and enthusiasm on the part of children and adolescents.
- Praise and encouragement are the best motivators concerning the setting of goals. Negative comments and the highlighting of mistakes are not understood by children the way they are meant and reduce the enjoyment of the game in teenagers.
- Critical comments should always be made on a one-to-one basis in as positive and matter-of-fact a manner as possible.

The Physical and Psychological Development of Children and Adolescents

Children are not "small adults". For this reason, training suitable for children and teenagers is not a simplified version of adult training. When coaching children and adolescents especially, the traits and characteristics of each of their respective stages of development should be taken into consideration. For this reason it is of prime importance to be aquainted with the characteristics of each individual stage of development and to dispense training in the appropriate quantities.

Child development is not a period of linear transition and growth. Rather, there are phases in which growth and maturity make great progress and phases in which development seems to stagnate. Each phase runs differently for different children; that is, in one child it starts earlier and later in another. This is also why relatively big differences can sometimes be observed in children of the same age. We therefore talk about biological and calendar ages.

Biological age orients itself to the physical development of a child or young person, which explains why an eight year-old may be as physically developed as a ten year-old, for example.

For the Junior Coach it is very important to know exactly at what stage of development his charges are in order to be able to offer the appropriate training. However the coach must creat specific training stimuli in every stage of development, as his charges have an increased learning capacity in given stages and react more intensely to certain exercise stimuli. In this way, a more rewarding learning success may be achieved.

In his book "Ausdauertraining" (bvl, 1988, p. 179), Fritz ZINTL says on this subject that, "Every stage of development has its biological peculiarities and priorities regarding the trainability of our stamina and co-ordination. Some of the known characteristics of different age-groups are that:
-   the early school years (ages 6/7 – 10) are an ideal time for the aquisition of motor skills and the improvement of co-ordination skills;
-   the later school years (between age 10 and the onset of puberty: age 11-12 for girls and age 12-13 for boys) are the best age for learning the specific practising of basic sporting techniques;
-   puberty (ages 13/14 for girls and 14/15 for boys) and adolescence (between ages 13-14 and 17-18 for girls and 14-15 and 18-19 for boys), is a very good time to develop the stamina because of the spurt in physical growth."

The various phases of development can not be clearly separated from each other chronologically since the transition from one phase to the other is fluid and is determined by the age of the individual. Research in developmental psychology has produced a whole series of graduated models, of whom the most important advocates/supporters are O. KROH, C. BÜHLER, W. ZELLER, A. BUSEMANN, PIAGET, NEUMANN and MÖCKELMANN, to name a few. We have decided in favour of a 3-stage model because
-   it appears sufficiently differentiated to show the necessary theoretical background on the one hand, and
-   there is enough room for practical application on the other hand.

Age/Stage of Development	Training Aim	Training Emphases	DFB-Divisions (of the Federal German Soccer Federation)
Ages 5-10 primary school	Soccer is fun	Basic sports training, track-and-field sports, gymnastics, ball-games, getting used to handling a ball, basic soccer techniques	Midgets Junior F's Junior E's
Boys, 10-12/13 years; girls, 10-11/12 years. Prepubescent phase.		The best ages for learning, training in playing and practice techniques	Junior D's
Boys, 12/13-14/15 years; girls, 11/12-13/14 years.	Improving our soccer-playing.	Separate types of training to take account of different rates of increase in height, consolidating techniques. Initial phase of puberty.	Junior C's, possibly Junior B's
Boys over 15; girls over 14. Second phase of puberty.	Playing competitive soccer.	Competition training, refining techniques, developing a personal style	Junior B's Junior A's

Planning Aids for the Designing of a Training Unit

Before presenting the following training units for the individual age-groups, we would like to introduce a practical and manageable system for the setting-up of a training unit.

At the same time coaches should not lose sight of the fact that, in reality, there will be constant alterations and postponements. The following 3-part division has proved successful:
1.   Getting going/warming-up;
2.   The main training section;
3.   Winding down.
When designing the content of each of these stages, certain guiding principles must be observed.

1. Getting Going/Warming-up

The beginning should be strongly motivational and should create the prerequisites for the following physical efforts. The warm-up should start with exercises of gradually increasing intensity, avoiding any rapid loosening-up exercises, to prevent any irritations or pulled muscles or tendons. Any already developed and hence familiar exercises, such as skills-training and ball-control, for example, should also be included.

No stretching exercises should be carried out with the Junior F to Junior D age-groups. Physical exertion for the Junior C's to Junior D's should be presented as a form of game, thus slowly increasing the strain on the cardio-circulatory system.

2. The Main Training Section

The warm-up is followed by training in techniques and tactics. The players are now alert and receptive to the learning of new techniques or the improving or refining of those skills and tactics already learned such as exercises and games such as kicking, playing against a larger or smaller team, or combinations of these skills etc.

As concentration and attention-span diminish any further learning becomes more difficult and may then be followed by conditioning exercises.
    In this connection the following points should be observed:
-    Skills training always precedes conditioning-exercises, never the other way round, as the players are no longer receptive to the learning of new skills after intensive conditioning-exercises.
-    Speed-training precedes training in power and muscular endurance.
-    If possible, general endurance training should come at the end of the session.

3. Winding Down

Lastly, a training unit is rounded off with a game and winding down exercises. The winding down in the form of a game lets the players try out and apply what they have learned, e.g. techniques or tactics, depending on what priorities have been set. The players should also be made aware that winding down after the game fulfills an essential function.

This plan serves only as a rough outline. It goes without saying that especially in the main section (2. above), various aspects of training may be "moved around", depending on what has been learned during the last few games or because how the season has been divided up. Thus, in preparation for the new season, training in techniques or tactics may be omitted in favour of concentration on fitness training, for example. Again, a training unit might contain no fitness training to allow concentration on tactics.

It is up to the coach to make these decisions. Depending on what he has planned for the coming season and on the position of the unit in the annual training schedule itself, he must decide which priorities to set.

Training Times

Age-groups	Total Time	Warming-up	Main Part	Winding Down
Midgets Junior F's & Junior E's	approx. 60 minutes	10-15	25-30	20-25
Junior D's	70-80	15-20	25-30	25-30
Junior C's	80-90	15-20	25-30	30-35
Junior A's & Junior B's	90	20-25	30-35	35-40

3.1   Playing Soccer Is Fun (Ages 5 to10)

This section addresses the Midgets and the children in the Junior E and F grades, i.e. children between four and ten years of age. Anyone who closely observes children in this age-group will see that they often learn new skills at the drop of a hat. Carried over to the game of soccer, the available practice-exercises must match the childrens' stage of development and their expectations. This in turn means that the children join the club because they want to play soccer. They are aquainted with neither tactical playing nor is the player drawn into the team-effort. For them soccer means:

THE BALL GOES INTO THE OTHER TEAM'S GOAL.

Thus the learning and practising of soccer must be presented in ways that children recognise as soccer. In easily-understood games and competitions the children are made familiar with basic techniques. As the children become more familiar with the game, individual techniques are repeatedly taken up and refined.

Besides playing with the ball, there is a broad range of further sports activities available, that takes children's need for play and movement into account.

General Training Tips

The children receive a varied basic sports training. This takes place by means of running- and jumping-games with and without the ball, climbing on a climbing-frame and pulling themselves along while hanging from a thick rope, through relay-races and field athletics as well as games of catch.

Hopping and jumping improve speed and games using the childrens' own body-weight increase their physical strength. To learn skills such as ball control, passing the ball or kicking a goal, each child needs his own ball.

At this age tactics play a merely subordinate role, and the children should not be forced into the straitjacket of learning tactics. Rather they should learn how to run round on the field, cover other team members, stop the other side scoring goals, and other aspects of tactics themselves.

Even aspects of physical fitness hardly figure here, as there is no keeping most children down as long as they enjoy the game. Although childrens' circulatory systems can cope with physical stress and strain, endurance training is little use. The improvement in physical fitness takes place in game form and running relay races. Agility, reaction time and speed can be "trained" in a similar fashion.

If the team then plays soccer, the younger children should play in a different position in each training session.

If they do this, time will show which position a child prefers.

The Role of the Coach

There are a few things that the coach must remember when working with children of all age-groups:

- Children of this age learn by imitation. Showing the sequence of events in soccer by demonstration or doing them with the children is an unavoidable and very efficient way of training them to move correctly.
- Children do not want big lectures on soccer theory. They want to play and try out for themselves what they have been taught.
- Mistakes should be rarely corrected and should be done in such a way that it is a clearly positive experience for the child.
- Criticism or even abuse are bad forms of motivation. A child will never understand them, because he will think he has done his best.
- Children need praise, and an interesting and varied training session will inspire them.
- Every coach should know that he is an example for his little charges, and that everything he says and does will be carefully observed.

Key to Symbols Used in Diagrams of the Training Units

X △ □ ○	Player
X . △ . □ . ○ .	Player with ball
⊕	Coach
X. ~~~→	Direction taken by a player with the ball
X – – – →	Direction taken by a player without the ball
——→	Direction of the ball
⌒⌒⌒⌒⌒⌒⌒	Dribbling/Doing tricks with the ball
⇒	Goal-shot
⊦	Flag
▲	Triangle

Aims: Introduction to the game of soccer
Getting used to the ball; playing with the ball
Improving co-ordination

F1

5 min Getting into the Mood/Warming-up

Why do you want to play soccer?
What do you like about it?
How do you play soccer?
Who's already watched a soccer game
or played a game himself?

TIPS FOR THE COACH

Hold a brief introductory talk with the
children, exploring their expectations,
awakening curiosity and enjoyment.

20-25 Getting Used to the Ball

- Running slowly with the ball.
- Kicking the ball in a straight line.
- Kicking the ball around a cone.
- Kicking the ball and stopping
  when motioned to.
- Running quickly then slowly with
  the ball.
- Throwing and catching the ball.
- Bouncing the ball on the ground
  and catching it again.
- Rolling the ball ahead a little,
  doing a forward roll, then picking
  it up again.
- Throwing the ball through your
  own splayed legs, turning around,
  running after it and catching it.

- Each child should be given a ball.
- The children should be praised often.
- The coach does everything as well.

The children gain experience in ball-handling
as it rolls, jumps, changes direction etc.

20-25 Winding Down

- Who can run the fastest with the
  ball at one's feet through both
  goals, hold it in his hand and
  bounce it?
- The ball must be dribbled around
  all the marking cones.
- Who can kick the most goals in
  a set time?
- Who can kick the ball into the
  goal every time?

As many 1 m-wide goals as possible are set
up all over the length and breadth of half
of the playing field.

Final talk with the coach; the children must
be left with a positive feeling on leaving.

F2

Aims: Introduction to soccer
Getting used to the ball
Goal-kicking Improving co ordination

5-10 Getting into the Mood/Warming-up

- Repeating the exercises from the first session.
- Guiding the ball with the right or the left foot.
- Running in a circle with the ball e.g. in the centre of the field.

20-25 Goal-kicking

- The children should try to kick as many goals as possible into one of the goals. Who can kick the ball 30 times into the goal without missing?
- Let's kick a goal and try to stop the ball that's coming in our direction.
- Who can kick the approaching ball straight back into the goal?

20-25 Winding Down

- Who can hit the other ball lying in the goal?
- Who can kick as many goals as possible in five minutes?
- To finish off we will play a game of "Catch": several "Catchers" have to try to "tag" the other players.
  This game can also be played kicking a ball.

TIPS FOR THE COACH

Each child has a ball to himself.

Team-talk: "Who can remember what we practised last time?"
Method of instruction: demonstration and getting the children to follow suit.

Form two groups, each standing approx. 10 metres apart. Set up several marking cones symbolising goals between the two groups.

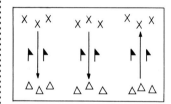

Form two groups as above and put an extra ball in every goal.

Change after 1 to 2 minutes.

Closing team-talk.

Aims: Introduction to soccer
         Goal-kicking (drop-kick)
         Improving co-ordination

F3

10 Getting into the Mood/Warming-up

Running with the ball at different speeds:
- Kick the ball just with your left or right foot.
- Kick the ball using the inside of your foot.
- Pick the ball up, throw it up into the air and catch it again.
- Pick the ball up, throw it into the air and then catch it again after it has hit the ground and bounced once.

20-25 Kicking Goals
- Who can kick the most goals?

- Let's run with the ball through a goal-post and back five times.
- Let's change the side the goal is on.
- Let's dribble the ball towards the goal, kick the ball through the goal, run around the outside and dribble the ball to the other side.

20 Winding Down

Today we are going to concentrate on relay games. Form several teams and run with and without the ball. We are going to start from the following positions:
- standing.
- sitting.
- lying on our stomachs.
- lying on our backs.

TIPS FOR THE COACH

Make sure that every child has a ball. The children should try out these exercises and invent different ways of handling the ball.

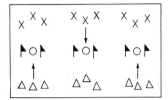

Two groups stand opposite one another, 10 metres apart, with a one-metre wide goal in the middle but this time with a goalkeeper.

Change the goalkeeper all the time. Due to the reduced effort required for this position, running- and catching-games should be included in the goal-kicking exercise.

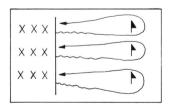

All teams should be of equal strength. Each team should win at least once.

F4

Aims: Getting used to the ball –
        Getting a feel for the ball
        Goal-kicking (kicking from a standing position)

10   Getting into the Mood/Warming-up

Running with the ball at various speeds
- Stopping the ball, then running with it in a different direction.
- Picking up the ball with both hands and then, as it falls, trying to kick it or lift it into the air with the thighs.

20-25 Goal-kicking

Two goals are set up 10 metres apart with a player in each.
- Each player tries to score as many goals as possible in the opposite goal. The player standing defence is allowed to fend off the ball as a goalkeeper would normally do.
- In a one-against-one game everyone has to act as a field player; defence with the hands is not allowed.

20-25 Winding down

This exercise focusses on catching the ball and getting it away from another player:
- "The Chain Gang": every player who loses the ball joins the other players. They all grasp each other by the hands, thereby forming a chain. This continues until all players have been caught out.
- Kicking-off and suddenly standing absolutely still in the kicking-off position.
- Running through a catching zone as often as possible.

TIPS FOR THE COACH

Make sure every child has a ball.
The children should also have a say by using familiar exercises to discover new ones.

The players form groups of two with one ball per pair. Practise goal-kicking and goal-defence in turn. The goals should be about 10 metres apart.

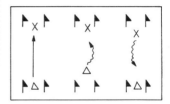

Goal- or corner-flags can be used as markers.

Aims: Getting used to the feel of the ball
        Goal-kicking and Goal-defence

F5

10   Getting into the Mood/Warming-up

We are going to dribble the ball past every one else all over the field and on my command, we are going to do a physical exercise as often as possible and then carry on dribbling the ball:

- Lie down on your stomachs.
- Jump up and clap your hands.
- Squat down.
- Hop forward in the squatting position.
- From a squatting position jump forward and do a half-turn.

20-25   Running with the Ball; Goal-kicking; Goal-defence

- We are going to dribble the ball across the field through the flags without losing control of it.
- When I call out, we are going to try and dribble the ball through all the flags.
- We are going to dribble the ball one-by-one through the flags and then kick a goal.
- Don't forget we also have to get the ball past the goalkeeper.

20-25   Winding Down

Now, we are going to try kicking goals between the goal-flags on a one-against-one or a two-against-two basis.

To finish off we are going to jog slowly once around the field touching all four flags. The players then jog slowly off the field.

TIPS FOR THE COACH

Make sure every child has a ball. Build a lot of physical exercises into ball control exercises. Each child could even be allowed to make up an exercise of his own and demonstrate it.

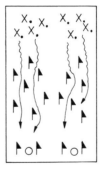

The playing field should measure 10 x 20 metres at the most, so that the running distance is not too great. The run is not a race and children should be able to talk to each other. The coach runs as well, and nobody is allowed to overtake him.

F6

Aims: Teaching a feel for the ball
        Dribbling and goal-kicking
        Heading the ball

10   Getting into the Mood/Warming-up

- Throw the ball up into the air and catch it again.
- Throw the ball up into the air, clap your hands and catch the ball again.
- Throw the ball up into the air and butt it with your head when it comes down.
- Throw the ball up into the air and but it several times with your head.

TIPS FOR THE COACH

Make sure every child has a ball. Exercises from previous practice sessions can also be worked into the current session.

20-25   Dribbling and Goal-kicking

- The object is to find the player who is best at kicking a goal from the 11 metres line
- Dribble the ball towards the goal and kick it into the goal.
- Run through a slalom-course with the ball and then kick it into the goal.
- The slalom-course consists of players, who have to stay where they are with one foot fixed to the spot when the player with the ball dribbles it past.

This exercise practises kicking goals when the ball is stationary. Every player has five turns. See who can score the most goals. Change the goalkeeper all the time, so that everyone has a turn as goalkeeper.

20-25   Winding down

- Finish off with a game of two against two, but kicking goals into the goal with a goalkeeper. The players change positions all the time. While leave the field the play run three times around each goalpost, starting from the kick-off point.

The goalkeeper hits the incoming ball as far away as possible with his hand. The goalkeeper must be changed all the time here as well.

Aims: Teaching a feel for the ball
          Heading the ball; goal-kicking

F7

10   Getting into the Mood/Warming-up
- Dribble the ball first slowly then quickly.
- At a sign from the practice coach, stop the ball as quickly as possible.
- Dribble the ball, stop it at a sign from me, lift it up with both hands, throw it up into the air and butt it with your heads.
- Dribble the ball, stop it at a sign from me, lift it up with both hands, drop it, lift it up with your feet again and catch it.

20-25   Heading the Ball/Goal-kicking
- The player throws the ball into the air with both hands, heads it, runs after it and kicks it at the goal.
- The player throws the ball up into the air with both hands and butts it with his head towards the goal. The distance between him and the goal must not be too great.
- The practice coach or a player throws the ball to one of the other players, who then heads it towards the goal.

20-25   Winding Down
This time we are going to play three-against three or four-against-four using two small goals (each about 1 m wide) and no goal-keeper. Both teams have to try and score a goal. Finally all players run one lap of the playing field and everyone is allowed to tell a good joke before leaving the field.

TIPS FOR THE COACH
Make sure every child has a ball. The ball is dribbled at random within a marked-out area of the field e.g. in the 16 metres area.

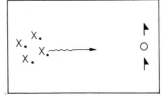

The players (between about 3 to 5) stand about 10-15 metres away from the goal. Soft balls should be used when practising heading.

Size of field: 20 x 15 metres.

The coach joins in and keeps an eye on the speed.

F8

Aims: Teaching a feel for the ball
Passing the ball with the instep
Improving co-ordination

10   Getting into the Mood/Warming-up

- Repetition of the exercises from previous training sessions.
- Shadowing your opponent: one player dribbles the ball all over the field and tries to shake off the player following him. Now change!
- Two players run all over the field and pass the ball to one another.

20-25 Passing; Goal-kicking

- One player passes the ball to his partner. This can be done in various styles.
- We are going to pass the ball through a 1-metre goal to our partner.
- We are going to play one-against one. All goals on the field can be used for this exercise.

20-25 Winding Down

- Who touched all the flags and made it back to the starting line first?
- Each player is allowed to start running relay-fashion after the previous player has touched all the flags.
- Then everybody starts running touches all the flags and at each flag, performs an exercise.
- We are going to play in teams of three-against-three or groups of five-against-five using two small goals with no goalkeeper and try to score a goal without a goalkeeper.
- We are going to run down every line except the outside lines.

TIPS FOR THE COACH

Make sure every pair has a ball. The playing field is marked off, into a smaller area. If the children have a fair idea of their sense of speed this exercise can also be played as a hunting game.

The goals are marked out with flags on a smaller playing field.

The playing field must initially be made larger to avoid players colliding with each other. It can be made smaller later.

The race starts from a common starting line.

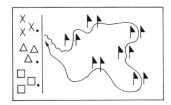

The coach runs at the head of the .group and sets the pace.

Aims: Getting used to the ball
         Exercises involving heading the ball

F9

10-15 Getting into the Mood/Warming-up

- In a separate, marked off part of the field between three and five catchers try to "tag" the whole team. The eliminated players squat down.
- The team plays "Chain Gang" (see explanation p. 22).
- "Shadow-running" without equipment: the leading player builds gymnastic exercises into the game.

20-25 Heading the Ball

- The players dribble the ball anywhere within the playing field and pass it to one another.
- The players pass the ball to one another. The player with the ball lifts it up and throws it to his partner so that the latter can head it back.
- The practice coach calls a player by name and throws him the ball. The player has to head the ball back. "Who can score the most goals out of five attempts while a goalkeeper is guarding the goal?"

20 Winding Down

- We are going to play in groups of four-against-four or six-against-six. This game can be played with or without a goalkeeper.
- When the training-unit is over, we are going to try winding down by running for three minutes without stopping, but in a totally relaxed fashion.

TIPS FOR THE COACH

This breaks down the initial overactivity. Alternatively, the "tagged" players can be relieved by the others.

Get the players to form pairs, with a ball for each pair. If possible the ball should be soft. Make sure that both players have the opportunity to head the ball.

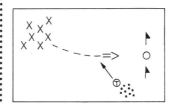

Goals scored by heading the ball count double.

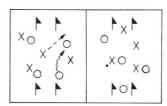

F10

Aims: Improving the feel for the ball
Dribbling
Improving co-ordination

10-15 Getting into the Mood/Warming-up

- "We are going to dribble the ball all over the field." "Let's try changing direction" (in soccer this is known as feinting).
- "We are going to kick away our partner's ball with our own ball."
- The coach calls out a number. All the children have to dribble the ball into these zones as quickly as possible and, once there, carry on dribbling so as not to hinder any other players.

TIPS FOR THE COACH

Make sure every player has a ball.

The playing field should be divided into four zones.

20-25 Dribbling and Guiding the Ball

- The whole group is divided into four teams. Each team stands in one zone. The ball is played between all players but the following tasks must be carried out:
- At a sign from the coach dribble the ball into the next zone;
- The players chase each other around all the zones;
- The players in zone one swap with those in zone two, zone three with zone four etc.
- The coach calls out a zone-number and all players in this zone dribble their ball towards a goal with a goalkeeper and, one after the other, try to kick a goal.

Players and playing field as above.

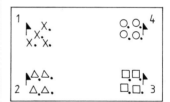

Four more goal areas, each with a goalkeeper, are set up in each corner of the field.

20   Winding Down

Competitions between partners
- "Who can pull his partner over the line?"
- "Who can wrestle his partner off his stomach and onto his back?"

Goal-kicking in teams of four-against-four or six-against-six using two goals. Everybody then runs in a crooked line for five minutes before leaving the field.

All players form pairs. One player grasps his partner over a line and tries to pull him over. He does this three to five times, then his partner has a turn.

The coach takes the lead.

 апреля

Aims: Improving a feeling for the ball
Strengthening co-ordination
Developing an understanding of the game
Kicking with the instep

F11

10-15 Getting into the Mood/Warming-up
- The team plays German Tag* on a field marked out with flags. Whoever is "knocked out" can rejoin the game if he hits another player with the ball.
- Keep the field clear: Which team had the fewest balls in its territory after five minutes?
- Now we are going to play rugby. You can touch the ball with your hands as well as your feet and everyone has to get it across a line.

20-25 Passing the Ball; Goal-kicking
- Any combination of several players on a smaller field.
- The ball is passed between two players who are running in a forwards direction.
- Each pair takes up position 20-30 m in front of the goalposts. Two players run towards the goal passing the ball from one to the other and then, at a given point, kick it at the goal.
- The above exercise can also be carried out with three players.

20-25 Winding Down
To finish off, the team plays a soccer game over the whole playing field, using two junior-sized goals, with and without a goalkeeper. Everybody does three laps of the playing field before leaving.

TIPS FOR THE COACH
Two teams are formed on a playing field of about 10 m x 10 m.

Have as many balls as possible on the field. The playing fields should be about 10 m x 10 m.

The players form pairs, with a ball for each pair.

Set up two junior-sized goals.

---
* "German Tag" is a game of "Tag" in wich one player with a ball tries to "Tag", or hit another player with the ball, thus getting him "out". The "tagged" player now has the ball and must try to "Tag" yet another plyer and so on.

F12

Aims: Getting used to the ball,
Improving mobility, dexterity
and co-ordination

10-15 Getting into the Mood/Warming-up

- Ball control exercises in a marked off area.
- The players change their speed all the time during these exercises.
- During ball control exercises players feint constantly by changing direction.
- The players throw the ball up into the air and stop it with one foot. They also practise receiving the ball.

20-25 Agility and Co-ordination

- The players bounce the ball with the right or left hand.
- The players bounce the ball around their bodies.
- The players throw the ball up into the air through their splayed legs over their backs and catch it again.
- The players stand on one leg, throw the ball up into the air and catch it again.
- The players bounce the ball while hopping on one leg.
- The players squeeze the ball between their feet, jerk it up into the air with a jump and catch it again.
- The players lift the ball with one foot.
- The players juggle the ball, even if it touches the ground several times.

20-25 Winding Down

- The ball is thrown to each member of a group of five players (1-2-3-4-5-1) in turn and then again in reverse order.
- Wind down with a game between two teams.
- Everybody finally takes five minutes to jog of the field in a relaxed fashion.

TIPS FOR THE COACH

Every child should have a ball.

Form groups of five players and number them all the way through.

Aims: Teaching a feel for the ball
         Circuit-training with emphasis on ball-techniques

F13

10-15 Getting into the Mood/Warming-up
- The players practise various exercises.
- The ball is passed over greater distances.
- Each player in the pair without a ball stands on the field with legs apart. The remaining players kick the ball between the legs of their partners. After every successful goal-kick, another attempt at goal is made in the same way.

20-25 Circuit-training: Ball-handling
1st *stage:* the 11 metre champion: who can kick the most goals in ten minutes?
2nd *stage:* each player plays one-against-one for five minutes.
3rd *stage:* the players kick the ball through a maze of plastic triangles with their feet, keeping it under control.
4th *stage:* the partners throw the ball to each other and the one catching it heads it back.
5th *stage:* the members of each pair kick the ball 20 times through a one metre wide goal post from a distance of 10 metres.

20-25 Winding Down
Training finishes with a game using the whole field. The size of the field should correspond to the children's age-group.
Finally all players jog twice round the field in an easy and relaxed manner. The winner of the games run in a clock-wise direction and the others run in an anti-clockwise direction.

TIPS FOR THE COACH
Form pairs, with a ball for every pair.

After a given length of time the players change positions.

There should be 2-3 children at each stage.

The ball should not touch the triangles.

After five turns the players change positions. The number of turns and times for each stage can be fixed.
Each pair has to pass through each stopping point.

F14

Aims: Running with the ball and dribbling
         Passing the ball with the instep
         Improving speed, reaction-time etc

10-15 Getting into the Mood/Warming-up

- "Day and Night": The "Day Team" stands about 2 m apart facing the "Night Team." The practice leader then calls to one of the two teams, which then has to catch the other team.
- Both teams first lie on their stomachs.
- They then lie on their backs. This is the starting position for the game.
- Both teams sit back-to-back.

20-25 Running with the Ball; Dribbling

- The first man dribbles the ball around once and the back to the relay-team, gives the ball to the next player and so on.
- A small goal is set up on the course. The player dribbling the ball pushes it through the goal, runs past, dribbles it around the marker and runs back.
- During the next run the player has to perform a forward roll.
- This time the player is allowed to dribble the ball with his weaker leg.

20-25 Winding Down

The game continues, but with four goals. Goal posts are set up on every side of the playing field. Each team thus has two goals to defend and can kick goals in two places. This time the players form pairs and jog slowly together while talking to each other for about 5-7 minutes before leaving the field.

TIPS FOR THE COACH

Two groups are formed on a playing field about 30 x 15 m large.

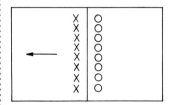

Two relatively small teams of 3-4 players are formed so that the waiting periods are not too long.

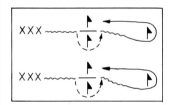

Four goals must be set up, one on each side of the field.

Aims: Improving teamwork
         Improving passing
         Improving basic techniques

F15

10-15 Getting into the Mood/Warming-up

Kicking the ball over the playing field.
A player throws the ball as far as possible.
His partner catches it and throws it back.
Who can force his partner back to the
baseline?

- This can also be played as a team
  game. The player who catches the ball
  also has to kick it back.

20-25 Improving Teamwork

- The players form groups of five and
  perform various exercises.
- The ball is then passed in a previously
  determined order.
- When playing four-against-one on a
  field 10 m x 10 m, four players pass the
  ball to each other. The remaining
  player tries to touch the ball. If he
  succeeds, he moves into the quartet.
- Playing four-against-one, throwing the
  ball with the hands.
- The game works similarly with five or
  six against two players. The members
  of the larger group have to pass the
  ball to each other, without the man on
  defence being able to touch the ball.

20-25 Winding Down

Two teams play to one goal. After each
goal the goal-kicker has to reinforce the
other team. Finally the players leave the
field in a crooked line, the man at the head
changing every 15 seconds.

TIPS FOR THE COACH

Have players form pairs and give every pair
a ball.

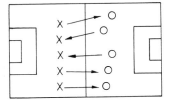

Make sure every group has a ball.

The game can also be played with three or
five-against-one, according to ability.
The players change position as soon
as the man on defence touches the ball.

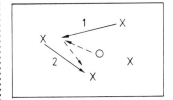

Aims: Kicking with the instep
         Catching and running with the ball

E1

10-15 Getting into the Mood/Warming-up

- The players start with a relaxed trot, then guide the ball along with the right or the left foot.
- They then juggle the ball with their feet. The players take the ball in their hands, throw it gently up into the air and butt it.
- The players take the ball in their hands, throw it gently into the air, catch it with their feet and run with it.
- The players take the ball, throw it gently into the air and "kick" it up again with their thighs.

20-25 Kicking with the Instep

- The members of a pair kick the ball back and forth to each other with their instep.
- As above. After each player catches the ball, he dribbles it around a plastic triangle before continuing as above.
- Holding the ball in his hand, one player kicks it to his partner, who catches it on his chest or with his feet.

20-25 Winding Down

Firstly the team plays a back-and-forth relay game with double passing of the ball. Then comes a final 7-minute run off the field with every player kicking a ball.

TIPS FOR THE COACH

Each player has a ball.

The players practise these activities with the ball on their own. The range of activities should be varied.

Pairs are formed, each with a ball.

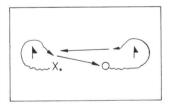

At this point the emphasis is on passing, catching and playing the ball cleanly.

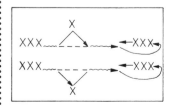

E2

Aims: Kicking with the instep
Stopping and controlling the ball

10-15 Getting into the Mood/Warming-up

- Throwing the ball in the air with one hand and stopping it with the foot.
- Throwing the ball as above and stopping it with the sole of his boot.
- Throwing the ball as above and stopping it with the instep.
- Throwing the ball as above and stopping it with the chest.
- Kicking the ball, working feints into the movements.

20-25 Kicking with the Instep

- The players stand opposite each other and play the ball to each other using their insteps.
- One player throws the ball from a distance to his partner, who catches it, kicks it a few metres along the ground and then throws it back to his partner.
- The players practise kicking the ball with the instep in various ways: with the ball at rest and in motion.

20-25 Winding Down

In a two-team game using two goals, the players pay attention to clean passing, precise playing and catching the ball.
Each player dribbles the ball slowly during the final five-minute run off the field.

TIPS FOR THE COACH

Every player has a ball.
The exercises should be carried out with both feet.

The players form pairs, each with a ball. This exercise can also be carried out by kicking the ball over a greater distance with the instep.

Aims: Kicking with the instep
         Teaching agility
         Improving playing techniques

E3

15-20 Getting into the Mood/Warming-up
- The players practise on their own with ball in order to improve the techniques learnt in previous sessions.
- The players juggle the ball with one foot, their head, thighs etc.
- The players throw the ball in the air with their feet or hands and stop it again.
- Passing the ball at varying speeds, while changing direction at the same time.

20-25 Improving Playing techniques
- Four or five players play against two in a marked off section of the field, either with unlimited or limited ball contact.
- This is followed by a game of four players against four using four goals.

20-25 Winding Down
To finish off, everybody plays „German Tag" (see p. 29).After the game the players can jog slowly off the field talking amongst themselves.

TIPS FOR THE COACH
Make sure each player has a ball.

Through his own example the coach gives the players further encouragement.

The larger team has to pass the ball as often as possible without a player from the other team touching it.

Each team has two goals to defend and can kick goals into any one of the two others.

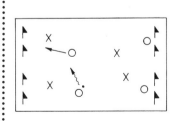

Each playing field can be 10 m x 10 m.

E4

Aims: Improving kicking with the instep
        Improving playing techniques

15-20 Getting into the Mood/Warming-up

- Shadow your partner: player A runs ahead. Player B follows him with the ball. Player A suddenly stops, stands still with his legs apart and Player B kicks the ball between his partner's legs, who then sprints after the ball.
- The players try to play the ball to each other standing about five to ten metres apart.
- Player A juggles the ball while Player B does 5 long-jumps. They then change places. Other possible exercises are: forward rolls, jumping up and down like a jumping-jack, jumping while carrying out a 180° or 360° turn or press-ups.

20-25 Improving Playing techniques

Everybody plays a tournament, with

- One-against-one, each trying to get the ball into one of two small goal.
- two-against-two as above.
- Four-against-four as above.
- Eight-against-eight, using the whole field and trying to kick the ball into one of two junior goals.

20-25 Winding Down

Everybody tries to kick the ball into one of two goals. Finally all players relax by running around the field for ten minutes.

TIPS FOR THE COACH

Each pair of players has a ball.

Depending on the skills of the players, the ball may first be stopped briefly before it is returned.

Playing time at every stage takes about five to seven minutes. Then the teams change by breaking up the old ones and forming new ones.

Aims: Improving basic techniques.
Improving playing techniques

E5

15-20 Getting into the Mood/Warming-up

- The players practice on their own with the ball.
- The players kick the ball ahead and sprint after it.
- The players run slowly while holding the ball in the air.
- The players kick the ball into the air and then catch it.
- The players kick the ball into the air, and, as soon as it lands, run on with it.

20-25 Improving Basic Techniques Using Circuit-training

1st stage: One player throws the ball to his partner, who catches it, runs a few paces back etc.

2nd stage: Each player kicks the ball with his instep to his partner from a great distance.

3rd stage: Each player dribbles the ball and then kicks a goal.

4th stage: One player throws the ball to his partner, who heads it back.

5th stage: One-to-one with two small goals but without goalkeepers.

20-25 Winding Down

A final game on the whole of the field. Each shot at goal wins one point, provided it does not go any further than five metres over or to the side of the goal area. Every saved goal wins two points and every goal ten points. Finally everybody jogs round the field for about five minutes to loosen up before leaving the field.

TIPS FOR THE COACH

Make sure every player ha s a ball.

Form pairs, one ball per pair. At each stage, each pair can practise about five minutes. If each pair runs the whole course in five minutes, the time should be halved.

If each pair practises for five minutes straight at any given stage, there should a "half-time" break.

E6

Aims: Improving teamwork
Improving ball-techniques

10-15 Getting into the Mood/Warming-up

- "Atoms": The players run all over the field at random. The coach calls out a number and the players form groups corresponding to this number as quickly as possible.
- "Stealing Tails": Each player has a ribbon with his team colours on it jammed into the rear of the waist band of his shorts. He has to try and steal everybody else's ribbon and defend his own.

25-30 Teamwork

- The players pass the ball to each other in a previously determined order (1 after 2 after 3 after 4 after 1 etc). This order can, of course, be changed.
- The game is played four or five against one. If the defender touches the ball, he changes place with another player.
- Four players play against four others in a limited space. Each team has to try to gain possession of the ball as often as possible. The ball changes possession all the time.

20-25 Winding Down

We play with two teams on a learners' field on which there are a lot of little 1m goals, each of which can be used for goal-kicking. Each team can kick goals until they lose the ball to the other team. Everybody runs off the field in pairs, passing the ball to each other.

TIPS FOR THE COACH

Various games and relays as a light-hearted introduction.

Form groups of four or five.

The number of players on the team playing against the defender is determined by the level of their ability.

Set up at least six to eight little goal-flags.

The players form pairs, one ball per pair.

Aims: Improving goal-kicking techniques
         Improving ball control

E7

10-15 Getting into the Mood/Warming-up

- The players kick the ball with the right or left foot, the inside or outside of the foot, in a circle, straight ahead or through a labyrinth of triangles
- The players throw the ball lightly into the air and stop it with their thighs or feet.
- The players throw the ball gently into the air, head it forward and then do exercises with it using their feet.

25-30 Goal-Kicking Techniques

- The players form groups of three or four and kick goals with the ball while it is resting motionless on the ground.
- The players dribble the ball towards the goal from directly in front, from the left or the right.
- The above exercises are carried out with both feet.
- Each player plays the ball with his instep to his partner, who then kicks to goal with either the inner or outer edge of his foot.

20-25 Winding Down

The team plays in small groups using two separate goals. The players should take care to spread themselves well over the field. After the game the players run around the field for five minutes talking with one another.

TIPS FOR THE COACH

Every player has a ball. They improve their ball control and agility through constant practice. Praise the players and their achievements repeatedly. The coach shows how this is done and then does the exercises along with the players.

The main emphasis is on the goal and goal-kicking. The players kick in the direct several flag-goals. The goalkeepers are changed all the time so that everyone has a turn.

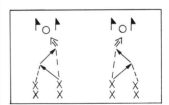

Note: Not everybody should run after the ball. Give tips on how the field should be divided up.

E8

Aims: Improving ball techniques
Improving basic techniques

10-15 Getting into the Mood/Warming-up

- The players practise by themselves: "What can you do with the ball?"
  The players perform familiar exercises and try to invent new moves with the ball. "Who can invent the most original exercise?"
- The coach observes the players at work. As soon as he sees that a player has invented a new exercise, he has the player demonstrate it. Everybody else copies it.

TIPS FOR THE COACH

Every player should have a ball.

If the players cannot think of any new exercises, he tries to give them some ideas by showing them some tricks himself.

25-30 Teamwork

- The players throw the ball to each. other.
- As above. After the ball has been thrown, the player performs a gymnastic exercise e.g. a forward roll, head-ball leap, or a leap from a squatting position ("jumping jack").
- The ball-passing is now interrupted by a defence player.
- The players form two teams. There are no goals. Every pass is worth a point.
- A game of indoor handball follows on a small area of ground. This time all goals count for points.

The players form groups of four, five or six.

Every group is given a handball.

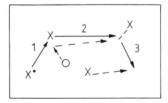

20-25 Winding Down

Finally the teams play a game of soccer with two goals and the usual rules. Each team finally jogs around its own half of the field, passing a ball from player to player before leaving the field.

This requires a proper football.

Aims: Ball control
        Improving teamwork

E9

10-15 Getting into the Mood/Warming-up

Each player practices the following exercises alone with the ball:
- Running with the ball.
- Changing direction while running with the ball.
- Stopping the ball with the sole of the boot.
- Stopping the ball in various situations.
- Throwing the ball in the air and heading it.

TIPS FOR THE COACH

Each player is given a ball.

20-25 Teamwork

- The players try to pass the ball directly to one another.
- Which pair or group can make the most direct passes?
- The group tries to keep the ball in the air. In the preparatory phase the ball is occasionally allowed to fall to the ground.
- This is then followed by games of five-against-two or six-against-two.

Each player passes the ball to his partner with his instep.

This is carried out in groups of up to six players.

20-25 Winding Down

This begins with a tournament on "mini" playing fields, with every team playing against the other.

e.g. one against one,
two   " three,
two   " four
three " four
one   " four
one   " three
Winning or losing is not important in this instance.

While leaving the field, the members of each team pass the ball to each other.

E10

Aims: Improving ball control and teamwork
         Improving basic techniques

10-15 Getting into the Mood/Warming-up

The players practise on their own with the ball doing gymnastic exercises as well:

- Running with the ball and doing forward rolls.
- Dribbling the ball and doing push-ups.
- Kicking the ball ahead and then sprinting after it.
- Kicking the ball up in the air, doing a forward roll and catching the ball again.
- Keeping the ball in the air using the feet, thighs and head alternatively.

25-30 Basic Techniques

These are improved at six separate stages:

- One player throws the ball in to his partner, who catches it.
- One player throws the ball to his partner, who stops it cleanly with his foot.
- One player throws the ball to his partner who heads it back.
- Two goals stand opposite each other, 10 metres apart. Using his instep, each player tries in turn to kick the ball into his partner's goal.
- In a one-to-one game the players try to kick goals into their opponent's goal.
- Long-distance goal-kicking competition or partners kicking the ball.

20-25 Winding Down

Two teams play against each other. Every player in each team is given a number. If a player scores a goal, he changes with the player in the other team with the same number. Finally the players jog off the field running with the ball through a labyrinth of plastic triangles. This takes several minutes.

TIPS FOR THE COACH

Every player should have a ball.

Everybody forms pairs, with a ball for each pair. Depending on the number of players, each stage may have more than one pair on it at any given time.

Aims: Improving ball technique
          (ball control)

E11

10-15 Getting into the Mood/Warming-up

The players practise by themselves with the ball:

- Dribbling with the right foot then the left.
- Throwing the ball up and catching it.
- Throwing the ball up, catching it on the thigh and "kneeing" it up again.
- Making up and trying out their own feints and tricks.

25-30 Ball Control in Relay-form

- Relay race with "slalom-dribbling" round flags.
- Pass-dribble relay: the players dribble the ball through the flags slalom-style then kick the ball against the wall, catch it again and dribble it back.
- Goal-dribble relay: the players dribble the ball through the flags slalom-style, pass ther ball through the goal, run round the outside, catch it with their feet and dribble it back again.
- Dribbling relay: each player dribbles the ball around each flag.

20-25 Winding Down

Next comes a soccer game without goalkeepers in which the players form small groups and try to score goals.
Everybody runs off the field along one of the sidelines.

TIPS FOR THE COACH

Every player should have a ball.

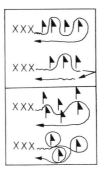

Do not make the groups too large.
Change groups frequently.
This game can be played on an individual or group basis.

E12

Aims: Playing games to improve the players' overall fitness
Improving technique and agility
Improving the players' feel for the ball

10-15 Getting into the Mood/Warming-up

- Controlling the ball with the right and left foot and with inside and outside of each foot.
- Controlling the ball while running through a curve.
- Controlling the ball while running in a figure eight.
- Building feints and deceptive manoeuvres into ball control.
- One player tries to kick the ball away from his partner, at the same time retaining possession of his own ball.

25-30 Playing Games to Improve Physical Fitness

- "Stealing the Ball": there are as many balls as possible in the middle of the field. One team guards them, the other tries to steal them and get them into one corner of the field.
- "Hens and Hawks" *
- Numbers Race: the players whose names are called run from various positions (standing, kneeling, sitting etc) with or without the ball around the turning marker (a flag) and back to their places.
- "Catch Your Partner" with role-change: every catcher gets a partner whom he has to catch. At a sign from the coach, the players change roles.

TIPS FOR THE COACH

Every player shold have a ball.

Which team can steal the most balls in a given time? This game should take last 3-4 minutes.

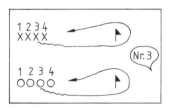

The ball may be dribbled, bounced, hurdles may be set up and gymnastic exercises included. If this game is played in groups of three. Every player has an active pause.

---

*   In "Hens and Hawks", all the players – except for the "catcher" or "hawk" - stand in a line one behind the other with their hands on the hips of the player in front. The player standing in front is the "hen", who stretches out "her" arms to protect the "chicken" standing at the end of the line from the "hawk". The hawk then tries to tag the chicken by running past the hen, avoiding her by twisting turning as necessary. The whole line helps the hen by running and turning in order to make it more difficult for the hawk to catch or touch the chicken. If the chicken at the end of the line is touched or tagged, he changes position.

E12

20-25 Winding Down

Everybody plays "German Tag" (see footnote on p. 29), at first with one ball, then with two softballs, then with barriers in each field. Everybody jogs along all the lines on the playing field while leaving.

3.2 Improving Our Soccer Playing (Ages 10 to 14)

Building on the first phase the improvement of playing techniques for 10 to 14 year-olds is now of prime importance. In this age-group especially the knowledge of the principles of neuro- locomotor and biological development respectively gains particular importance. After childhood, 10-14 year-olds go through a further period of maturation.

The Prepubescent Phase

The phase between primary school age and the onset of puberty is referred to as the pre-pubescent phase. For boys this phase lasts from age 10 to age 12-13; for girls it is usually completed a year earlier.

"In this phase childrens' height and breadth increase at a more or less constant rate, and their body organs adapt to this progressive development. This results in harmonious and smooth movements." (c.f. W. MAIER, Leistungsfußball)

MEINEL describes this phase in his theory of movement as the best learning phase. Movements can be learned very quickly and often instantly. Children at this age do not think about things for too long but try movements in the order they are demonstrated, and after only a short period they are capable of understanding this. This is the reason that the improvement of soccer techniques should be emphasised in the practical part of training. These techniques should not be worked on and consolidated in isolation but in a corresponding game-environment. For this reason training in techniques should always consist of two aspects:
• Frequent and concentrated repetition, in order to make movements come automatically (the interplay of the central nervous system and the muscles).
• Technique training requires orientation in a game whereas skills in individual game-situations need to be practiced (in other words, you learn to play soccer by playing soccer).

General Training Tips

In the area of the rudiments of technique the whole range of of techniques should now be taught, practiced and applied. Thus, the various goal-kicking techniques should be refined, for example. In this connection equal facility with both feet should be aimed for. Equally, the "heading" of the ball should be improved and made more accurate. If noticeable errors occur, the coach should make a point of correcting them.

Rudimentary tactics should also be targeted. The players learn basic tactics by playing in a wide variety of games. Here the one-against-one up to eleven-against-eleven models present themselves.

Basic tactics mean: goal-kicking, dribbling, ball control, teamwork etc.

New developments also become apparent in the area of physical fitness. At ages 11 to 12 the best prerequisites for training in endurance and speed are present. The improvement of co-ordination, mobility and agility should also be aimed at otherwise these abilities become stale or even diminish. Long-distance runs lasting five, seven, ten or even fifteen minutes, during which the players talk with each other, can be included here. Sprints lasting ten to fifteen metres with active recovery stages in between are inherent requirements for the game.

Horst DE MARÉES found that from about age of ten, children begin to adapt to the demands of endurance training, but separate fitness training is not necessary. In this age-group the inclusion of these exercises in the game is of prime importance.

The Role of the Coach

For children of this age-group the coach should be capable of demonstrating techniques to the children during game situations. His stock of games and training exercises should be varied and imaginative. His increased assistance and correction must be given in an empathetic manner. Praise and encouragement are also positive reinforcers of the learning process.

The First Stage of Puberty

With the onset of puberty childrens' bodies change shape. The beginning of the increase in height indicates to the coach that the players' successful learning period is now at an end. As a result of the rapid growth in height an imbalance in the relationship between the length of the legs and the torso develops, so that movements appear uncoordinated. With increased growth in height, it is more difficult to learn the sequence of movements and those basic techniques already learnt must be reinforced. The introduction of new technical sequences is difficult and not necessarily to be recommended, because too little progress is made in learning (this is crisis period for the motor system). The relatively considerable differences in growth rates must be taken into consideration by means of different types of training for each individual player. A height-difference of 20-30 cm (in the C-Grade players, for example) between the biggest and the smallest player in the team is not uncommon.

General Training Tips

For this age-group there is a clear need for exercises that refine and improve technique.

Here these techniques should be practised and reinforced under better conditions. The learning of new technical sequences brings little success. At this stage the intellect begins to develop. From about age twelve the memory reaches its highest degree of receptiveness.

The coach should make use of this in tactics training. The fundamentals of tactics can be worked on in simplified form in the Junior D's. Now, in the Junior C's, more difficult tactical matters can be acquired. The players can discover and try out tactical solutions for themselves through play and co-ordinate their own playing behaviour with their fellow-players and opponents. This can be practised in games where one team has more members than the other or in standard situations and their variations.

Conditioning now plays a greater role. Aerobic endurance and speed can easily be trained. Endurance training now makes games over a longer period just as possible as runs of 10 to 15 minutes in length with and without the ball. Children may be easier to train with the onset of puberty, but power-training before this stage is of little use.

At the same time neither extreme strength training nor endurance training should be carried out. Strength training is confined here for the future to-tug-of war games, jumping exercises and so on.

It can also be carried out using the player's own weight, light sports equipment, a medicine ball or a rope. Circuit-training is also suitable for this age-group. Regular training in manoeuvrability and agility should also be continued. Speed training, carried out by means of games of reaction or by sprinting, is highly effective.

The Role of the Coach

In this age-group the coach requires special sensitivity for his task.
- He should fulfill the adolescents' wish for, and aspiration to, independence.
- He should accept the adolescents as independent pesonalities. (The players no longer want to be children.)
- The coach should be an expert and specialist on the one hand and show himself to be an understanding friend on the other.
- At this stage adolescents react particularly sensitively to criticism and they require special attention. For this reason one-to-one talks and personal attention are preferable as a means of communication.
- The coach should not set himself up with an exaggerated authority for the adolescents.
- He must be involved in non-sporting activities and social activities and organise other forms of events for adolescents.
- He should have a sense of humour and be capable of having a joke with adolescents.
- His goal should be to gradually educate adolescents to a sense of personal responsibility and give them the freedom to try out things for themselves.
- The coach should motivate and encourage adolescents with praise and personal talks.
- He needs much patience with adolescents.

Summary

This second training section (for 10-14 year-olds) has a special importance as in no other phase of development is the deviation so obvious apparent or extreme as in the group of the Junior C's and D's.

For this reason exercises must be made available on an individual basis. The coach must divide the groups up and offer different tasks for the various stages of development according to different physical requirements. Activities that overtax a "little" thirteen year-old represent a lack of challenge for a "big" thirteen year-old. In order to achieve the right amount of physical exertion for everybody the coach needs good pedagogical and organisational skills.

Important: Training designed to optimise performance alone will only challenge those players who are physically more developed i.e. the big, strong players. But no-one can tell whether these "early developers" will be among the top performers later on when their physical advantages are equalled by the later development of the "little" players. At this age the performance-lead is chiefly a development margin and no proof of great talent. Favouring such early developers when designing training is irresponsible and could arguably foster the wrong players.

Aims: Improving technique
         Teaching co-ordination

D1

15-20 Getting into the Mood/Warming-up

- The players trot in a relaxed fashion around the playing field.
- Skipping and running, hopping on the right, then the left foot, hopping, "ski-jumping", running and twisting to the right and left, running backwards and forwards, five sprint bursts and jogging backwards.
- The players practise with the ball by themselves: juggling, feinting and general ball techniques.

25-30 Improving Techniques

- Keeping the ball up in the air.
- One partner throws the ball up, the other heads it back.
- One player passes the ball to his partner, who runs towards it.
- Catching the ball after one player calls out to his partner (ball control)
- One-against-one without a goal.

25-30 Winding Down

- A game with six-against-six or seven-against-seven (without goalkeepers) with flagged areas marking two goals.
- Everybody jogs around for five minutes before leaving the field.

TIPS FOR THE COACH

It is assumed that a 15-20 m length of field is available for the exercises.

After the sprint the players should trot in a relaxed fashion. Every player should have a ball.

The players form pairs, with a ball for each pair.

This should be practised with both feet from the start. Between each of these demanding exercises there should be an active pause.

D2

Aims:　Improving technique
Goal-kicking: one-against-one

15-20 Getting into the Mood/Warming-up

The players practice with the ball by themselves:

- Dribbling with both feet.
- Kicking the ball into the air and controlling it.
- Throwing the ball up into the air heading it, sprinting after it and bringing it under control.

TIPS FOR THE COACH

Each player should have a ball.

25-30 Goal-training

- Running from the centre line, picking up the ball and kicking a goal.
- The coach stands on the centre line, each player of the pair on either side of him: the coach kicks the ball, both players sprint after it to get control of the ball and kick a goal.
- One player stands behind his partner. Partner A opens his legs, Player B kicks the ball through Player A's legs, both race after it and try to score a goal.

The players form pairs with a ball for each pair.

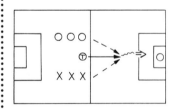

25-30 Winding Down

- Teams of six-against-six or eight-against-eight are formed. One team tries to kick the ball into a goal marked by flags set up on the side of the field, the other tries to kick the ball into a normal goal with a goalkeeper.
- Finally the players wind down by jogging for five minutes before leaving the field.

The players change positions after 10-15 minutes.

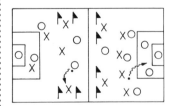

Aims: Improving techniques
         Speed training

D3

15-20 Getting in the Mood/Warming-up
We start at warm-up speed with:
- Passing.
- Dribbling.
- Ball control together with gymnastic exercises such as:
- Squats.
- Press-ups.
- Forward or backward rolls.
- Jumping up and "heading" the ball.
- Jumping and making a full turn before landing.

These exercises can also be carried out in groups of two, allowing time for a break.

25-30 Speed training
- One player juggles the ball in the .air, while his partner does a sprint. The players then change positions. After 4-5 sprints, the players have an active break, such as playing with the ball on their own.

- One player kicks the ball about 10 m and 45° to the right and to the left while his partner standing opposite chases after it and kicks it straight back. (see diagramm above right.).

25-30 Winding Down
- The players form two teams and play a game of soccer using two goals.
- All the players wind down by taking five minutes to jog off the field.

TIPS FOR THE COACH
Get the players to form pairs, with a ball for each pair.

After the ball has been passed or kicked once, the players perform an exercise at a signal from the coach.

The players form themselves into groups of two. The distance to be sprinted should be about 10-15 m long.

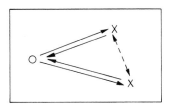

After the players have done this 5-8 times, they change positions, during which the players can take active breaks.

D4

Aims: Improving techniques
         Getting a better feel for the ball
         Improving teamwork

15-20 Getting into the Mood/Warming-up

- Games of Catch.
- The "Chain Gang."
- The players occupy themselves with the ball as follows:
- Dribbling the ball for short distances with both feet, keeping it under close control.
- Dribbling the ball at varying speeds.
- Dribbling the ball, feinting and changing direction.

25-30 Teamwork

This consists of various types of passes:

- 4-against-1 on a field of reduced size.
- 3-against-2: the object is to dribble the ball over each base line.
- 2-against-2: two players try to kick the ball into a goal marked out by several flags and defended by a goalkeeper.

25-30 Winding Down

The training unit should end with a soccer game using two goals. After the game all players jog for 5-7 minutes before leaving the field.

TIPS FOR THE COACH

This exercise is designed to break down initial hyperkinesia.

There should be one ball per player. After 1-2 minutes there should be an active break.

Each exercise should be repeated 3-5 times.

Form groups of five players with one ball. The other four players try to get by with as little ball contact as possible.

After a few minutes the teams should be reshuffled as playing in groups of two is very tiring.

The game is played over the length or the width of the field.

Aims: Improving techniques
         Improving speed

D5

15-20 Getting in the Mood/Warming-up
- .Kicking the ball in a circle in the centre of the field.
- The four corners of the field or shorter distances are given numbers. The coach calls out a number and all the players dribble ball in this direction and back again.
- As above. The players sprint to the corner but dribble the ball back slowly.
- The players now play "Come with me! Run away!" – with and without the ball. (A game in which the players call to their team-mates to run after them and then run away.)

25-30 Improving Speed
- Two players (A and B) stand about 20 m apart with a third player (C) between them with the ball. Player C dribbles the ball to Player A or passes it to him in a series of leading and catching moves.
- Start as above, but the player in the middle only plays continuously for 30-45 seconds: C dribbles the ball to A, kicks it to him, A lets the ball rebound, C takes the ball, turns around and dribbles it to B and so on.

25-30 Winding Down
Two opposing teams play a soccer game with two goals and two goalkeepers.
After each goal scored, another player acts as goalkeeper. Finally all players jog around the field for five minutes.

TIPS FOR THE COACH

Every player should have a ball.

The distances and running speeds should correspond with the ability of the players.

Form groups of three, with a ball for each group.

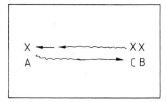

Always build an active break in between the exercises, to be arried out in several series.

D6

Aims: Kicking techniques
         Improving teamwork

15-20 Getting into the Mood/Warming-up

- On a divided playing field 2-3 catchers try to tag as many players as possible. Every tagged player continues playing. Which catcher can tag as many players in a given time?
- As above, but with one condition: nobody may be tagged when he lifts both feet of the ground.
- As above, except that 3-4 more balls are used. Whoever has a ball at his feet cannot be tagged.

25-30 Kicking-techniques

- The players pass the ball using the outside and inside of the foot while on the move.
- One player drives the ball over the whole length of the field. Which partner can force the other player back over the base line? This exercise can also be carried out as a group exercise.
- Each player kicks a football hard to his partner, who tries to catch it.

TIPS FOR THE COACH

This exercise is designed to break down initial hyperkinesia.

After 30-45 seconds, choose new catchers.

Or when lying on his stomach, doing a handstand or "sitting on his hands".
(A player sits on the ground. His legs are bent and may not touch the ground. His arms are allowed to rest on the ground.)
Pay attention to teamwork and skilful passing.

Every two players should have a ball.

One player shoots the ball out of his hand with a hard blow (this may need to be demonstrated). His partner tries to catch it or receive it and shoots it back from that point.

This is carried out in pairs.

D6

25-30 Winding Down

- "Catch 10": Which team can pass the ball ten times between its members without the other team touching it?
- The players play a soccer game diagonally across the width of the playing field.
- The players jog around the field for 5-7 minutes.

The team with possession of the ball passes it between its members and the other team tries to touch the ball. Every pass made without the other team touching the ball is worth a point.

D7

Aims: Improving the feel for the ball
Improving teamwork

15-20 Getting into the Mood/Warming-up

Everybody plays with the ball on his own with the aim of improving his technique:

- Juggling the ball.
- Tossing the ball up in the air and catching it again.
- Dribbling with both feet.
- Practising heading the ball.
- Practising feinting.

30-40 Improving Techniques with Circuit-training

Six different practice points should be set up on the playing field:

1st stage: One player throws the ball to his partner, who heads it back.

2nd stage: The players try to keep the ball in the air.

3rd stage: One player throws the ball to his partner, who catches it cleanly.

4th stage: Each player drop-kicks the ball into the goal.

5th stage: At a distance of about 10 m each player kicks goal-shots into a 1 m-wide goal marked by flags.

6th stage: Slalom-dribbling.

20-25 Winding Down

The players play a game of soccer on the whole area of the field.

Finally they jog slowly off the field.

TIPS FOR THE COACH

Each player has a ball.

These exercises should be completed in pairs.

The exercises at each stage should last 3-4 minutes. An active break can be worked in between each different stage.

Both players pass the ball to each other.

Aims: Improving techniques
and teamwork

D8

15-20 Getting into the Mood/Warming-up
- Moving with the ball on a smaller field.
- By deliberately kicking the ball along the ground, one player tries to knock out the balls kicked by other players.
- The players kick the ball with one foot then the other at varying speeds.

30-40 Improving Ball Techniques with a Partner
- One-against-one duel: one player kicks the ball at his partner, who tries to block it each time with his body. There are no goals.
- One player throws the ball to his partner using the "throw-in" technique. His partner plays with the ball while it is still in motion.
- A player throws the ball to his partner, who jumps up to head it.
- Each pair juggles the ball in the air with their feet, thighs, head etc.
- One player passes the ball to his partner on the move.
- Both partners run a 10-15 m sprint race with the ball and then jog back slowly.
- Each partner dribbles the ball with the top of the foot between toes and ankle, then kicks a goal. This is done with one foot, then the other.

25-30 Winding Down
Finally, everybody plays a tournament on mini-sized field. They then take several minutes to jog slowly off the field.

TIPS FOR THE COACH
Each player should have a ball.

Each player should have a ball.
Each exercise should last about 3-4 minutes.

Two-against-two or three-against-three using two little goals marked by flags. After five minutes the teams change members, so that everybody can play against everybody else.

D9

Aims:　Improving techniques

15-20 Getting into the Mood/Warming-up

Back-and-forth relay races with the ball:
- One player dribbles the ball to his partner, gives him the ball and goes and stands at back of the line.
- The players run through a slalom-course.
- The players have to carry one or two medicine balls as well.
- At certain positions the players perform gymnastic exercises.

30-35 Improving Techniques

- The players play one-against-one and try to kick the ball into one of two small goals.
- Each pair performs a duel by heading the ball. The two players stand about 5 m apart. One player throws the ball up into the air and heads it into the goal.
- Two players playing against each other run all over the field throwing the ball at each other using the "throw-in" technique.
- Two players throw a ball to each other. Each player has to catch it safely.
- Each pair juggles the ball. After being touched three times at the most it must be passed to the other partner.
- One player has a shot at goal from the dribble. After about seven shots the goal-kicker changes position to become goalkeeper and vice-versa.

30-35 Winding Down

This starts with back-and-forth relay races, while player simultaneously dribble a ball. A game of soccer diagonally across field then follows.
Finally the team jogs slowly off the field.

TIPS FOR THE COACH

Several relay teams stand opposite each other, about 10-15 m apart.

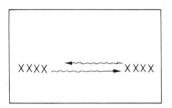

Each exercise lasts about 3-5 minutes. The active break should not be forgotten.

The winning relay team has to run 1 m longer.

Aims: Improving techniques under
competitive conditions
Improving teamwork and tactical playing

D10

15-20 Getting into the Mood/Warming-up

The children work with the ball on their own. They practise previously learnt exercises and think up new ones.

30-45 Soccer Tournament: Consolidation of those Techniques Already Learned.

Those techniques already learned are now put into practice:

- One-against-one games with mini- goals.
- Two-against-two as above.
- Four-against-four as above. (The goals should be marked with small flags.)
- Eight-against-eight, as above, using goals of a size appropriate for school-pupils

15-20 Winding Down

Today's training unit is concluded with exercises with one's own partner:

- "Cockfighting".
- One-to-one fights standing on one leg.
- Tug-of-war.
- Press-up fights: the partners lie next to one another and each partner tries to throw his opponent onto his back. Finally everybody jogs around the field for five minutes.

TIPS FOR THE COACH

Each player should have a ball.

Playing time is about 3-5 minutes per game, after which the partners should be changed around. The playing field should be enlarged according to the number of players.

For these games the players play across the width, rather than the length, of the field.

These one-to-one exercises are fun, strengthen the muscles and teach agility.

D11

Aims: Improving technique at the various stages around the field;
Teaching tackling.

10-15 Getting into the Mood/Warming-up

Each player practises on his own with the ball:

- Dribbling.
- Controlling the ball with both feet at varying speeds.
- Kicking the ball up into the air and playing with it.
- Practising deceptions and feints.

25-30 Improving Techniques

- The players play the ball through a slalom-type course, dribbling it with both feet, and with the inside and outside of each foot.
- The players juggle the ball with their thighs, head, heels, keeping it in the air.
- Each player takes ten shots at goal while the ball is stationary on the ground, using first the right foot, then the left foot, from about 11 m.

20-25 Winding Down

The players practise the following skills using the whole area of the field:

- Double passes.
- Goal-kicking, including with the weaker foot.
- Carrying the ball with the thigh and head.
- Dribbling the ball for at least 10 m.

TIPS FOR THE COACH

Each player should have a ball.
The coach provides encouragement by doing the exercises himself.

The players carry out these exercises for five minutes at each stage. The whole group should be divided into two teams. One team completes the course while the other plays one-against-one soccer using mini-goals.

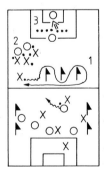

Aims: Improving teamwork
         Improving Goal-kicking techniques

D12

10-15 Getting into the Mood/Warming-up

- Each pair practises double passing, long-distance passing, close-up passing.
- While practising the above, 2 or 3 players disrupt the exercises all over the field.
- Which pair can be the first to make ten direct passes?
- Which "disrupter" is the first to intercept ten balls?

25-30 Goal-kicking and Teamwork

- Player A dribbles the ball from centre line to the goal-area followed by Player B. A pretends to make a pass, but butts the ball back with the sole of his foot to B, who kicks a goal. After each turn the players change positions.
- A passes the ball diagonally towards the corner flag. B races after it, butts it back with his foot and A kicks a goal.
- A stands 20-25 m in front of the goal and receives the ball from B. A takes it, turns around briefly or dribbles it for a short distance and then makes a goal-shot.
- A stands 20-25 m in front of the goal and receives the ball from B. He gets ready to kick a goal, and B dashes behind him in an attempt to get the ball from him.

20-25 Winding Down

To finish up, the team plays a tournament in small groups. Then everybody jogs slowly off the field in pairs.

TIPS FOR THE COACH

The players form pairs with a ball for each pair.

Peripheral vision is called for here to keep an eye on the disruptive players.

Clean, precise passing to one's partner is required.

These exercises should also be carried out with both feet.

The correct timing of each pass is important here.

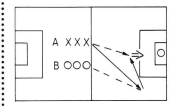

Aims: Techniques and goal-kicking
         Dribbling and aspects of physical fitness

C1

15-20 Getting into the Mood/Warming-up

- "Catching In Threes": The players get together in threes, numbered from 1 to 3. Player No. 1 catches Player No. 2 while No. 3 has a break. No. 2 then catches No. 3 and has a break and so on.
- Mixed exercises in groups of three as follows:
- Any combination of exercises.
- Passing the ball in a set order.
- After passing the ball, the players either jump up into the air as if to head the ball or perform a 360° turn or perform a press-up.

TIPS FOR THE COACH

The players form groups of three. The playing area is restricted and physical contact is not allowed.

25-30 Goal-kicking from a Dribble

- The players dribble the ball from the centre line and then kick goals from the penalty line.
- As above. The player who has just kicked a goal stands on the 16 m line. After the double pass and goal-kick this player then changes position to become the player who passes the ball to the player kicking the goals.
- As above. The "passer" kicks the ball back and then becomes an opposing player.

All players require a ball and should be taught to kick goals with both feet.

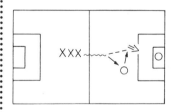

30-35 Winding Down

Finally the teams play seven-against-seven or eight-against-eight on the whole area of the playing field. Goals scored by means of a double pass count double. The players dribble the ball while jogging off the field in order to learn spatial orientation. The players should try to avoid bumping into each other.

Every player should have a ball.

C2

Aims: Improving teamwork
Improving physical fitness

15-20 Getting into the Mood/Warming-up

- The players practise playing in teams of uneven numbers e.g 3 against 5. The frequency of ball contact is fixed according to the ability of the players.
- In these games emphasis can be put on limited ball contact, use of the full width of the field, making double-passes and playing on both wings etc.

25-30 Physical Fitness

The players jog in pairs over a small-sized field in a relaxed fashion. Player A throws a medicine ball to Player B, who catches it and throws it back.

- Each pair uses the medicine ball to practise throwing-in.
- One player throws the medicine ball between his legs to his partner.
- Each player passes the ball to his partner and then does either press-ups, a short-distance sprint, squats, or long-jumps, forward-rolls etc.
- One player throws the medicine ball up into the air. Each player tries to catch it on the way down before his partner does.
- The whole team plays "Tussle-Ball" * on a small-sized field.

30-35 Winding Down

A soccer game then follows using the whole field. The players then take 7-8 minutes to jog slowly off the field.

TIPS FOR THE COACH

The players improve their general physical condition by working with a medicine ball in pairs. Every pair should have a ball. The exertion involved in this should last 1-2 minutes.

When these exercises are completed, each pair kicks goals into a small-sized field. Then follows the next round exercises.

---

*   In "Tussle-Ball", two opposing teams on a smaller field try to get a medicine ball into the other team's goal or across their opponents' line. The ball may be rolled, carried, thrown or kicked. The player in possession of the ball may be blocked, stopped or held by his opponents, but if he loses possession of the ball, he must be let go. The ball is placed on the centre line at the start of the game and after each time a goal is scored. When the coach blows his whistle, both teams run from their goal line and try to gain possession of the ball. If the ball rolls "out", i.e. off the field, the team that was last in possession of the ball regains possession. Fouls like tripping up, hitting and unfair play are not allowed. In case of a foul, the fouled player gains possession of the ball. This game is very similar to rugby.

Aims: Improving general physical fitness
Improving combination games

C3

15-20 Getting into the Mood/Warming-up

- The players use the ball to practise changing direction, changing speed and close ball control on their own.
- All balls lie in a separate part of the field e.g. the penalty area. The players remain outside this area. At a sign from the practise coach, the first player runs up and touches all the balls with his hand. The other players follow suit.
- Starting position as above. The players then run up at the same time and touch all the balls with their hands.
- The same exercise can be played as a relay race.

25-30 Improving Physical Fitness and Teamwork

- Each player throws a medicine ball up into the air and catches it while jumping into the air himself.
- Keeping hold of the medicine ball, the players swing it back and forth between their legs and back in an arc.
- The players hop right or left over the medicine ball which is lying on the ground.
- The players jam the medicine ball between their feet, jerk it up into the air and catch it with their hands.
- The players throw the medicine ball backwards through their legs and over their backs and catch it as it passes over their heads.
- Everybody plays 4-against-4 or 5-against-5.

30-35 Winding Down

Everybody then plays a soccer game over the whole area of the field and then jogs off the field for eight minutes.

TIPS FOR THE COACH

The players sprint from ball to ball.

The players switch between the fitness exercises and goal-kicking into mini-goals. The individual exercises with the medicine ball last about 1-2 minutes.

This game supplements the exercises to improve the players' physical condition.

C4

Aims: Improving techniques (dribbling, Cross-passing the ball), Goal-kicking

15-20 Getting into the Mood/Warming-up

The players form pairs and concentrate on practising feinting, other deceptions and passing over long and short distances.

TIPS FOR THE COACH

Every pair should have a ball.

25-30 Cross-passing the Ball and Goal-kicking

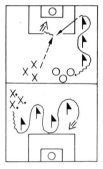

- Partner A dribbles the ball through a slalom-course, cross-passes the ball to Player B, who tries to kick a goal. The passes can be made with the head or the feet.
- As above, but this time several attacking players stand in front of the goal, who also want to score a goal.
- This time the player dribbles the ball through a slalom-course and then kicks a goal. All exercises should be carried out with both feet.

30-35 Winding Down

The teams plays a game of soccer on a mini-sized field with flags marking the oal and no goalkeepers. The tournament goes from two-against-two to three-against-three to four-against-four. After the tournament the whole teams jogs off the field.

The number of players in every team is changed every five minutes.

Aims: Improving ball-handling techniques
         Reinforcing teamwork

C5

15-20 Getting into the Mood/Warming-up

- "Hand-and-Head-Ball" with two goals. The ball is passed with the hands, but the goal must be scored using the head.
- "Hunter and Prey" *. Depending on the size of the groups, three to five players are designated as "hunters". It is their job to "knock out" or tag the others. Any player who is hit becomes a "hunter".

25-30 Improving Playing Techniques and Tactics to Promote Teamwork

- The players pass the ball to each other with their instep, the inside and outside of their foot.
- The players pass the ball on in a pre-determined order and may touch the ball as often as they like before they pass it onto the next player.
- Player No. 1 throws the ball to No. 2, who heads it to No. 3, who catches it and throws it to No. 1 as though he were throwing it in and so on.
- The players practise one-plus-one-against-one on an open field. The emphasis is on free ranging.
- Two-against-one on a smaller field. The players change positions each time the ball is touched.
- The players play two-against-one and try to score goals into a mini-goal marked by flags. After each goal, the players change positions.

30-35 Winding Down

The players play games in groups according to their ability on a mini-field. They then jog for eight minutes before leaving the field.

TIPS FOR THE COACH

Alternatively, the players may not carry the ball in their hands while running. When playing on a mini-field, the 16 m area is usually sufficient.

The players form groups of three, with a ball for each group.

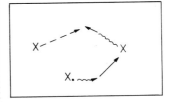

This exercise requires one player to pass the ball, one to attack and one to defend. The attacking player tries to shake off the defending player by deceptions and rapid starts. He then passes the ball to the attacker, first with a forward pass, then with a backward pass.

---

* "Hunter and Prey" is a German ball game in which two players try to tag the other players or get them "out" by hitting them with the ball. Those players which are hit become "hunters".

C6

Aims: Improving techniques and tactics
Improving physical-fitness with games

15-20 Getting into the Mood/Warming-up

- Each player practises on his own with the ball.
- This is followed by a "pass-and-sprint" relay. Team A forms a lane and the members pass the ball directly to each other. Every pass counts. Meanwhile a player from Team B sprints around the entire field. The object is to see how many passes Team A can make before all the members of Team B have run around the field. The teams then change position.

25-30 Improving Techniques and Tactics

The players form three teams (A, B and C) with three members each. This game requires two small goals.
Team A plays against Team B and Team C always plays with whichever team possesses the ball, so that six players always play against three.

- The larger team is only allowed to make one or two passes.
- Let's see how long the larger team can hold its own!

30-35 Winding Down

To wind down the players run relay races. These may be quite funny e.g. if each player has to dribble two balls at once. The jogging off the field at the end should not be forgotten.

TIPS FOR THE COACH

Each player is given a ball.

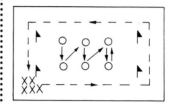

A variation of the game is to set time limits to these activities. The teams should change position frequently and there should be breaks between each activity.

The players form groups of nine.

Other combinations of players are possible which means that the number of players is important.

This can be played either as oneway or there-and-back races over 10-15 m.

Aims: Improving aspects
         of physical fitness

C7

15-20 Getting into the Mood/Warming-up

- Each player practises with the ball: changing direction, feints, changing speed, kicking the ball with either foot.
- "Shadow-Dribbling" in groups of two, with regular position changes.

25-30 Improving Physical Fitness and Teamwork

- Partner A bends forward with his feet apart. Player B jumps over him and then crawls between his legs. They do this 5-10 times before changing position.
- Both players sit back-to-back with their arms entwined. Each player tries to pull his opponent onto his side.
- Player A leapfrogs over Player B and crawls between B's splayed legs. They do this 5-10 times. They then change positions.
- Both players practise "Cossack-dances" from a crouching position, holding their partner's hands.
- Both players then practise cockfighting.
- Blocking passes: on a smaller area of the field the players pass the ball to each other. Depending on the number of players 3-5 players, recognisable by their jerseys, act as blockers and try to prevent the pairs from passing the ball to each other.

30-35 Winding Down

The players finish up with a soccer game using four goals. They then jog for five minutes before leaving the field.

TIPS FOR THE COACH

Each player should have a ball.

Each pair should have a ball.

These exercises can also be done on a circuit.

The players form pairs, each with a ball. This exercise practises keeping an eye on the whole game using peripheral vision. The players alternate constantly between exercises with a partner and blocking passes.

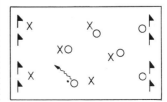

C8

Aims: Improving the feel for the ball
Improving speed with the ball
Dribbling

15-20 Getting into the Mood/Warming-up

- The players dribble the ball on their own.
- "Atoms": the practise coach calls out a number and the players gather in groups of that number.
- Shadow-dribbling: the player in front with the ball tries to shake off the player behind him (who also has a ball).

25-30 Improving Techniques and Speed with the Ball

The players practise the following exercises: kicking the ball with either foot, juggling the ball, feinting without body contact etc. At a sign from the coach, the players change quickly into the other area.

- Alternatively, the players form two groups. Each group practises in its own area and, at a sign from the coach, moves into the next area.
- Alternative No. 2: a narrow lane (3-4 m) between the two playing areas is marked with flags, through which the players have to dribble the ball when they change areas.
- Alternative No. 3: a group stands at each corner of the playing area and one group chases the other around the square-shaped area. This exercise can also be played in relay-form.

TIPS FOR THE COACH

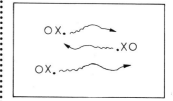

Two square areas on the field, each 10-15 m long should be marked out. Both areas should be about 30 m apart.

The players sprint 30 m to the other area.

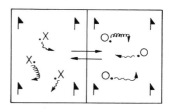

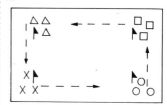

C8

25-30 Winding Down

Tournament: All players with first names starting with A to K play against those with first names starting with L to Z. If this makes for uneven numbers, the division must be made some other way. Finally everybody jogs slowly for eight minutes before leaving the field.

C9

Aims: Improving ball-handling
        Improving tactical playing

15-20 Getting into the Mood/Warming-up
The players start off with passing-games in pairs:
- Double passes.
- Kicking the ball from a distance, catching it and kicking it on.
- Players call for a pass by putting on a sprint.

40-50 Improving Tactical Playing
- The players play three-against-two or five-against-three with the following emphases for the larger team: limiting ball-control, direct passing, passing to the wing players taking into account the width of the field, making double passes. The emphasis for the smaller team should be: possession of the ball for as long as possible, each player retaining individual ball control, counter-attacking.
- The teams change positions after 5-10 minutes. Between each game there is an active break in which the players perform exercises with the ball e.g. keeping it in the air using their feet or heads, juggling etc.

20-25 Winding Down
The players finish off with a soccer game using the whole area of the playing field. This time the fair-headed players play against the dark-headed players. Afterwards, the training session ends with a jog off the field.

TIPS FOR THE COACH
Groups of two players are given a ball.

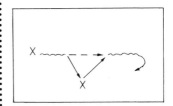

In games with teams of uneven numbers, the teams should be made up such in way that takes the size of the whole group into account.

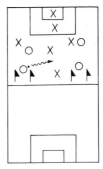

Aims: Practising Goal-kicking
         and goal-keeping

C10

15-20 Getting into the Mood/Warming-up

The players jog in a relaxed fashion over the field performing the following exercises:

- Relaxed jogging.
- Increasing speed.
- Increasing speed while sprinting.
- Performing a hop, skip and jump using the arms.
- Sprinting and suddenly making a 360° turn.
- Running backwards and forwards at a sign from the coach.
- Performing long-jumps.
- Hopping.
- With each alternate heel striking the buttocks while running.

25-30 Practising Goal-keeping

- In their capacity as right and left wings, Players A and B pass the ball to each other in front of the goal. The D-Players line up in front of the goal area and try to convert the passes into a goal.
- The same exercise can be performed with one or two defence players.
- The C-Players kick a goal. The D-Players try to divert the goalkeeper's attention.
- Finally the wing-players and the forward players alternatively kick goals from the centre and pass the ball from both sides of the field.

30-35 Winding Down

Everybody plays handball in small groups (four-aganst-four or five-against-five). Goals may only be scored by heading the ball. Finally everyone jogs around the field for eight minutes before leaving the field.

TIPS FOR THE COACH

While all soccer training for young people should emphasise use of the ball, it is perfectly in order to practise without the ball every so often, even for a few minutes.

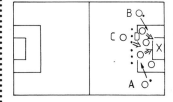

All goalkeeper training is also practised for the forward players and training in goal-kicking. The players pass ball at least ten times from each position before then changing positions.

C11

Aims: Improving group techniques

15-20 Getting into the Mood/Warming-up

The players divide up into several groups and play handball. Goals may only be scored by heading the ball. Each team could consist of between 4-5 players.

25-30 Improving Techniques in Pairs

Exercise 1: Juggling the ball – who can do it the best?

Exercise 2: One player dribbles the ball in zig-zag fashion while being shadowed by his partner. The players change positions after every round.

Exercise 3: One player throws the ball to his partner, who heads it back.

Exercise 4: Drop-kicking goals.

Exercise 5: Goal-kicking using the inside of the foot into a small goal as directly as possible.

Exercise 6: One player throws the ball to his partner, who kicks a goal by suddenly swivelling his hips and kicking from the side.

Exercise 7: One player throws the ball to his partner who catches it and runs with it.

Exercise 8: One player throws the ball to his partner as though he were throwing it in.

30-35 Winding Down

The training session should end with a soccer game using the whole of the play-field. The midfield players play against a combination of defending and attacking players. Finally everyone jogs around the field for 8-10 minutes.

TIPS FOR THE COACH

Each pair should have a ball, which they take from stage to stage. With large groups each stage should be capable of catering for two pairs at the same time.

Make sure the exercises are performed carefully and well. No pressure to compete should be exercised. Each exercise should last 3-5 minutes.

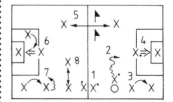

Aims: Improving general physical fitness
       Improving skill and agility

C12

15-20 Getting into the Mood/Warming-up

- The players practise various passing combinations while jogging slowly with the ball.
- Passing with the right and left foot.
- Passing with the inner and outer side of the foot.
- Double passes, catching the ball and kicking it on.
- Double passes, kicking the ball on immediately.

25-30 Improving Physical Fitness, Dexterity and Agility

- One player throws the medicine ball to his partner while both jog slowly.
- As above, but one partner catches the ball in the middle of a leap.
- A player throws the medicine ball to his partner as though he were throwing it in.
- A player throws the medicine ball to his partner backwards through his legs.
- A player jams the medicine ball between his feet and shuffles it over to his partner.
- A player passes the medicine ball to his partner and quickly performs a push-up or jumps up into the air as though he were heading the ball.
- Each pair plays "tag" with the ball on a small section of the field using a small goal-post.

30-35 Winding Down

A soccer tournament using smaller goal ends the training session. The goalkeeper of one team switches to the opposing team. Then everyone jogs around the field for 5-8 minutes.

TIPS FOR THE COACH

The players form pairs, with a ball for each pair.

Groups of two players practise together with a medicine ball. The exercises can be performed as a series of separate events.

3.3   Playing Competitive Soccer (Ages 14 to 18)

After puberty is completed, physical co-ordination techniques improve again. This second stage of puberty lasts about two years for boys between the ages of 15 to 18 and ends a year earlier for girls. A physical reharmonisation takes place: the growth in body-width catches up and the motor system works in a more co-ordinated fashion. The adolescent experiences a second "golden age of learning" in which new techniques, and moves for competitive sport are developed.

General Training Tips

In the area of techniques, games and exercises of a competitive nature are now offered, where the pressure of time and opponents are important. The players also practise techniques relating to specific positions. Here, accuracy and increasing speed are important. After all, this is where all techniques are perfected, and the search for a personal playing style begins.

In the area of tactics, the development and discussion of moves on video and the blackboard are used as well as on the training field. If the various theoretical aspects of tactics have already been developed, their practical application may now begin, which then promises greater success. Here, behaviour during tackling, speed changes and transfer play are practised.

If physical fitness is important, this can be begun from age 16, when maximal strength training can start as well (when the bones at the end of the spine have hardened). But static endurance training should be avoided here if possible. In the area of special strength training, speed, power training and endurance as they relate to soccer should be forced. Speed training at this age may thus correspond to that for adults. Particular emphasis must be put on training in speed endurance in order to bring the players up to top performance. In competitive soccer, special fitness training is necessary as from age 15. At this level, maximum physical fitness can only be trained through special fitness training. According to Gero BISANZ, not all necessary aspects can be trained to the required extent with soccer training of a purely fun nature alone.

The Role of the Coach

When dealing with people in this age-group, the coach must show adolescents that he is an experienced expert.
• It is important that he accepts the adolescents as individuals with their own personalities.
• The coach must pass on his responsibility to the players as far as possible.

- He should talk with the players e.g. about which tactics should be used in the next game.
- It is important for the players that the coach is available as an advisor when problems occur and has a good eye and an open ear for such eventualities.
- The coach must try to create a basically positive atmosphere in the team, especially when critical situations arise.
- If a player has come to the end of his time as a junior player, the coach must help him to transfer to a senior team.
- In this phase of development the player's personal style plays a greater role in the area of technique and tactics. The coach should encourage this development, but at the same time stamp out any mistakes, so that they do not take root.

Aims: Improving technical skills
         Improving tactical playing
         Practising goal attacks

B1

20-25 Getting into the Mood/Warming-up

- Various forms of passing.
- Juggling with the ball.
- Keeping the ball up in the air while performing a second exercise e.g. Player A juggles the ball while Player B sits down and stands up again, takes the ball from A, who then sits down.
- Kicking balls hard, with clean catching and continuing to run on with it.
- Player A always passes the ball, Player B dribbles it, while feinting and changing direction.

30-35 Improving Take-off Power, Practising Goal Attacks

- A hurdle course, consisting out of 5-7 hurdles about 1-2 m apart, is set up for either hopping over on one leg or jumped over in the usual fashion.
- The players play four-against-three, trying to kick the ball into a goal with a goalkeeper. Four attackers try to overcome the three defence players. Two small goals are set up on the centre line so that the defending players can also kick goals.

30-35 Winding Down

The exercises conclude with a soccer game over the whole of the field. The players practise the points covered above. The players then jog for ten minutes before leaving the field.

TIPS FOR THE COACH

The players form pairs, with a ball for each pair. Another variation is to jump up and head the ball, perform a press-up, a forward roll, dash around the flag and back etc.

After five attempts, the players change position.

The players should relax and stretch between individual exercises.

The height of the hurdles is determined by the players' ability. This exercise is also possible as a relay. Positions should be changed between exercises.

The attacking players should concentrate on double passes, dogging players from the opposing team, kicking goals from the second row. The defence should concentrate on taking over the covering of an attacking player from fellow team-members, the right dispersal of players on the field and countering the opposing team. The exercises should last about ten minutes.

B2

Aims: Improving basic physical fitness
Improving tactical playing
Practising goal-kicking
Outwitting the opposing team in order to score goals

20-25 Getting into the Mood/Warming-up

- The players throw a medicine ball up into the air while jogging slowly and catching it again.
- The players lay the medicine ball on the gound and jog slowly around the medicine ball labyrinth.
- The players throw the medicine ball up into the air, touch the ground with their hands before catching the ball again.
- The players jump over the medicine ball on one or both legs.
- The players stand with their legs apart, pass the medicine ball in a circular motion downwards through their legs and then up towards their backs and bring it back through their legs again.
- As above, except that the ball is thrown. The players then turn around and catch the ball again.
- "Catch": The players throw the medicine ball to one another in any order. One or more catchers try to intercept the ball and catch the other players out. Anyone possessing the ball cannot be caught out.

30-35 Practising Speed and Goal-kicking; Outwitting the Opposing Team in order to Score Goals

- Two players sprint in a parallel line from the centre line. The coach passes the ball to them and they both compete for possession. The successful player then kicks a goal.
- Two players run from the centre line parallel to each other in a slalom-like

TIPS FOR THE COACH

Each player should have a medicine ball.

The players should throw the medicine ball continuously and may not keep hold of it.

The players alternate constantly between exercises 1/2 and exercise 3.

B2

course to the penalty area, the coach passes the ball to them, they compete for possession and the successful player kicks a goal.

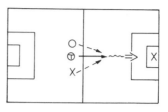

- Attack versus defence: three forwards and three backs play against three defending players and three backs, trying to kick the ball into the goal or into two smaller goals on the centre line.

20-25 Winding Down

The whole team plays soccer using the whole field, paying attention to the points to be emphasised above. Everyone then jogs around the field for 8-10 minutes before leaving the field.

The emphasis is on attack: effective combination, building up an attack, double-passing and goal-kicking.

Emphasis is on defence, effective marking and countering.

B3

Aims:	Improving techniques and a feel for the ball
	Improving tactical playing

20-25 Getting into the Mood/Warming-up

- Independent dribbling.
- Shadow-dribbling: one player dribbles the ball and another copies him e.g. forwards, backwards, sideways, jumping up and heading the ball etc.
- One player dribbles the ball and the whole group copies him.
- Chase: one player kicks the ball and shakes off his partner by changing direction.

TIPS FOR THE COACH

Every player should have a ball.

30-35 Dribbling

- The players dribble the ball in a smaller playing area.
- "Dribbling by Numbers": all four corners of the field are numbered. The coach calls out a number and all the players dribble the ball quickly around the flag in that particular corner and back.
- Chase: four teams chase the team in front around the smaller playing area.
- The players form groups of four. Every two players stand opposite each other, about 20 m apart with their legs apart. They then start kicking goals.

This can be performed individually or as a group competition.

The two non-active pairs play alongside on a one-to-one basis. After about 2-3 minutes they change positions.

35-40 Winding Down

Groups play four-against-three or five-against-three using two goals with goalkeepers. The larger team tries to score a goal with as little ball contact as possible. The smaller team tries to score goals by dribbling the ball. After the game the players run around the field for ten minutes before leaving the field.

Aims: Improving playing

B4

20-25 Getting into the Mood/Warming-up

To warm-up, everybody plays four-against-two or five-against-two on a smaller field.

30-35 Improving Playing

- The first game is played two-against-two plus one using small goals.
- The second game is played six-against-four without goals. The larger team may have contact with the ball up to three times. The smaller team has to dribble the ball for as long as possible i.e. keep it away from the larger team.

35-40 Winding Down

The training session ends with a soccer game using the full area of the playing field with the attackers now playing against the defending players. The team then jogs around the field for ten minutes.

TIPS FOR THE COACH

This exercise should be carried out with limited ball-contact and be based on the players' level of ability.

The neutral player always plays with the team possessing the ball. He can change sides every 5 minutes or so.

The teams change position every 10-12 minutes.

B5

Aim: Improving tactical playing

20-25 Getting into the Mood/Warming-up

- The players jog in a relaxed fashion first across then up and down the playing field.
- Stretching exercises.
- Running at increasing speeds.
- Co-ordination exercises, including "jumping jack".
- The players form groups of four, and pass the ball to each other. Individual players claim the ball by sprinting after it. They also kick the ball over long distances.

30-35 Tactical Playing

In teams of four-against-four the players dribble the ball over lines on a field reduced in size.

35-40 Winding Down

A soccer game using the whole field follows. This time the attacking players play in defence and the former defence players take over the attack. Finally they all perform loosening-up exercises while jogging around the field for about ten minutes.

TIPS FOR THE COACH

This time the players warm-up without the ball.

Each group should have a ball.

Each game lasts about five minutes. The players then have an active pause using the ball. The game provides for about 3-5 repetitions in all.

Aims: Improving the players'
         understanding of the game

B6

20-25 Getting into the Mood/Warming-up

- The players jog around the field passing the ball to each other.
- The players pass the ball to each other in a prescribed order.
- Get the players to pass the ball by putting on a sprint.
- Practise direct passes.
- The players kick the ball over longer distances to other team-members, who catch it as though it were a pass.

30-35 Tactical Playing and Teamwork

- In the first phase two players play two-against-two. The composition of the teams is decided by drawing lots.
- The players then play three-against-three using two small goals.
- When playing four-against-four, two teams from the first phase can each join forces.

35-40 Winding Down

The players now play six-against-six or eight-against-eight. The teams now have two normal goals with a goalkeeper but also a goal marked with flags but no goalkeeper. Afterwards everyone jogs slowly off the field.

TIPS FOR THE COACH

The players form groups of six, each with a ball.

The game lasts about 5-8 minutes and the break lasts 1-2 minutes. Each game is repeated three times.

The points for emphasis are determined by the findings arising from the last championship match.

B7

Aims: Improving tactical playing

20-25 Getting into the Mood/Warming-up

- Various exercises in groups with ball juggling in between.
- Relay races: e.g. a dribbling relay around a turning mark or through a slalom-course.

30-35 Tactical Playing

Groups of five play against each other. On each side there are three little goals marked by flags. Three players each defend one goal while the two remaining players stand in front of the defence chain as intercepters on the field. The object is to improve the covering of the field and accepting the ball by one player when passed by another.

35-40 Winding Down

The team then plays a soccer game using the whole field. The best players go into Team A, the not-so-able into Team B. During a game lasting with two halves lasting 15 minutes each, Team B receives a five-goal advantage. Finally everybody jogs off the field.

TIPS FOR THE COACH

The players form groups of five, with a ball for each group.

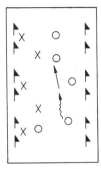

The coach interrupts the game and comments on the playing e.g. correcting, praising, clarifying etc.

The players should pay attention to tactics and the working out of new moves.

Aims: Improving speed with the ball

B8

20-25 Getting into the Mood/Warming-up

- Everybody plays in groups of five-against-two on a smaller field. There is as much ball contact as possible, then reduced ball contact and direct passing of the ball.
- "A Journey to Jerusalem". Each player has a ball. On the field stand triangles set out in a labyrinth and corresponding to the number of players. At a sign from the coach every player has to dribble a ball up to one of the triangles.

30-35 Speed with the Ball

- The players dribble the ball in a marked out section of the field. Several numbered flags stand about 20-30 m away. At a sign from the coach all players dribble the ball as quickly as possible around the flag indicated by the coach and back.
- "Dribbling Competition": the coach gets two players to complete the above course as a race.
- The same competition is now carried out as a relay race.

30-35 Winding Down

The team plays a game of soccer over the whole of the field and finally jogs around the field for ten minutes.

TIPS FOR THE COACH

Pay attention to the players' ability- level.

The number of triangles can be reduced. Whoever does not reach his triangle receives a minus point.

Each player has a ball.

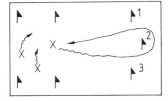

B9

Aims: Improving techniques

20-25 Getting into the Mood/Warming-up

- Groups of two players jog in a relaxed fashion, passing the ball to each other.
- Each pair juggles the ball.
- One player claims the ball from his partner by sprinting after it.
- The players stand back to back, legs apart, and pass the ball to their partner through their legs or over their heads.
- The players stand as above and pass the ball to their partners by swivelling their hips in a sort of rollercoaster fashion.
- One partner jams the ball between his feet and "flicks" it through the air to his partner.

30-35 Improving Techniques

- One player kicks the ball hard from a distance to his partner. The partner catches the ball and returns it in the same fashion.
- As above, except that the second players returns the ball by heading it.
- Player A stands on the 16 m-line. From a distance Player B kicks the ball to A, who receives it and turns around and kicks a goal.
- As above, except that Player A has to contend with a partly active player on goal defence. Player A receives the ball, feints and kicks a goal.
- As above. Player A bounces the ball from Player B. Both players now face the goal defence player in trying to score a goal.

35-40 Winding Down

The players play a game of soccer using the whole playing field. The emphasis is on "long passes". Finally they all jog around the field for ten minutes.

TIPS FOR THE COACH

The players form pairs, with a ball for each pair.

The players perform gymnastic exercises in pairs.

Both partners work together.

The ball can be thrown back depeding on the ability of the player.

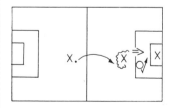

Aims: Improving technical skills
         Improving playing

B10

20-25 Getting into the Mood/Warming-up

- The players jog in a relaxed fashion practising various forms of passing
- Player A dribbles the ball to Player B, dribbles it around him, runs several metres with the ball and then passes it to B. A and B then change positions.
- Player A dribbles to the approaching Player B, who takes over the ball. The players then change roles and repeat the above.
- Player A dribbles the ball to Player B, who bounces it back (in a double pass) A then takes the ball back and repeats the aforegoing.

40-45 Improving Playing Techniques using Circuit-training

1st stage: Slalom-dribbling and then a goal-kick.

2nd stage: Two teams of three players each try to score goals using mini-goals.

3rd stage: Two teams try to score goals handball style and by heading the ball. This exercise requires two goal-posts, each with a goalkeeper.

4th stage: The wing players pass the ball sideways each other in front of a goal and then convert the passes into goal-kicks. Alternative: passes as above but the two wing players have to try and get the ball past a defending player into the goal.

20-25 Winding Down

Everybody plays a soccer game using the whole field. Finally everyone jogs around it before leaving.

TIPS FOR THE COACH

The players form pairs, with a ball for each pair.

.

After 5-8 attempts the players change positions.

6-8 players can play at each stage. The teams spends about eight minutes at each stage.

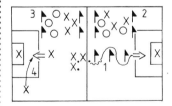

B11

Aims: Improving playing
Improving teamwork

20-25 Getting into the Mood/Warming-up

- Group-members pass the ball to each other practising all the varieties of moves they have learned so far.
- Passing receives special emphasis during practice.
- The group also practises direct double passes.
- They then pass the ball to each other and then performing a gymnastic exercise.

30-35 Improving Playing and Teamwork on a Circuit

1st stage: Each group plays three against-three using small goals.

2nd stage: four-against-two on a smaller field. The 4-man team may only have four contacts with the ball before each kick-off.

3rd stage: two-against-two on a revolving basis. Team 1 attacks, Team 2 defends. Once the attack is completed, Team 2 attacks and Team 3 defends etc. Alternatively, one player from the defending team goes into the goal, thus allowing a two-against-one-game.

30-35 Winding Down

The groups divide up into teams of six and begin a tournament, where every team plays against the other.

TIPS FOR THE COACH

The players form groups of six, with a ball for each group.

The players form groups of six again.

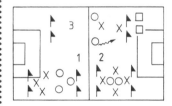

The teams change from stages 1-3 every 5-8 minutes. The three stages can be gone through more than once.

Aims: Improving ball-techniques
         Improving speed with the ball

B12

20-25 Getting into the Mood/Warming-up

Each players practises with the ball on his own, performing gymnastic exercises such as squats, heading the ball while jumping, jumping up and turning around on his own axis, press-ups, jumping jack, straddle-vaulting etc. Speed dribbling then follows on a separate field alternating with ball gymnastics every ten seconds. This change between exercises can be repeated up to ten times.

30-35 Speed with the Ball

Four 10 m x 10 m squares are staked out on one half of the playing field and numbered from 1-4.

- The players dribble the ball at a relaxed jog on the other half of the field. At a call from the coach everyone sprints into the numbered square he names. They then continue dribbling the ball until the next call.
- The players dribble the ball accordeon-style: They dribble the ball from the base line to the 5-metre line and back, then to the 16-metre line and back, then to the centre line and back, repeating this several times.

30-35 Winding Down

Two teams play a game of soccer over the whole area of the field. Goals scored by heading the ball count double. Finally everybody jogs around the field for 5-10 minutes before leaving the field.

TIPS FOR THE COACH

Each player has a ball.

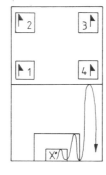

Aims: Improving goal-kicking

A1

20-25 Getting into the Mood/Warming-up

The players practise on their own with the ball:

- Kicking the ball with either foot and with the inside and outside of each foot.
- Juggling the ball.
- Throwing the ball into the air, heading it, running after it and working with it.
- Stopping the ball with the sole of the foot and then dribbling it further.
- Changing direction and speed while running with the ball.

30-35 Goal-kicking

- Goal-kicking from a dribble directly in front of to the goal and then diagonally from right and left.
- The coach stands in the 16-m area, a player kicks the ball in his direction, makes a double-pass and then kicks a goal.
- Players A and B stand on the centre line right and left of the coach, who kicks the ball straight ahead. A and B sprint after it, compete for control of the ball and the successful player kicks a goal.
- As above, but with a sprint through a slalom-course (marked out with stakes) as well.
- As above, but with a forward roll before sprinting after the ball.

35-40 Winding Down

The team plays a soccer game with two goals emphasising goal-kicking after competing for control of the ball from a fellow-player. If a player scores a goal in this manner, it counts double. Finally everyone runs a few laps slowly before leaving the field.

TIPS FOR THE COACH

Each player has a ball.

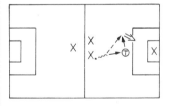

Special attention should be paid to this point during the game.

A2

Aims: Improving goal-kicking
Improving teamwork

20-25 Getting into the Mood/Warming-up

- Group-practice of various passing-moves at warm-up speed.
- Keeping the ball up in the air, juggling it etc.
- Group practice: various passing moves in a given order.
- One player calls for a pass from his partner by putting on a spurt.
- Active pause: juggling the ball again.
- Various passing moves at a relaxed speed after performing a gymnastic exercise.

30-35 Practising Goal-kicking and Teamwork

- The players play a game of soccer with uneven team-numbers all over the field. All players in the bigger team have to complete the next exercise one after the other before they are allowed to go on playing again. Once all players in the larger team are finished, they change positions with the smaller team.
- One member of the larger team must complete the following exercise: 10-12 balls lie on the 16-m line. The player kicks the first ball towards the goal and then sprints around a flag. He then kicks the second ball etc.

35-40 Winding Down

To wind down two teams, as far as possible of the same size, play a game of soccer. While running off the field everyone runs past every corner flag at least three times, but one flag after the other.

TIPS FOR THE COACH

The players form groups of four or five.

Player No. 1 passes the ball to Player No. 2, who passes it to No. 3, and then to No. 4 etc.

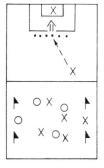

Aims: Improving tactical playing (teamwork)
         Improving tackling

A3

20-25 Getting into the Mood/Warming-up

- Ball control at slow speed. Ball control with changes of direction feints.
- Getting the ball up into the air, catching the ball, dribbling the ball.
- Everybody plays "Dribbling Knock-Out": everybody dribbles the ball. One player is designated catcher; he also dribbles a ball. When he knocks another player out, this latter player becomes catcher.

30-35 Teamwork and Tackling

- The players play one-against-one with one marked off goal and a goalkeeper. When somebody scores a goal, the goalkeeper changes places with a team-mate.
- The players play one-against-two with various moves on an open field, first with two contacts with the ball, then with a direct kick. If the single player touches the ball, he swaps positions with one of the other players.
- In the same game the ball is then dribbled along the sidelines.

35-40 Winding Down

Finally everybody plays a tournament on the small field with three-against-three. The players then jog around the field for ten minutes.

TIPS FOR THE COACH

Each player should have a ball.

The players form groups of three, with a ball for each group.

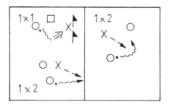

As groups of three have already been formed, these can continue here.

A4

Aims: Improving physical fitness using the ball

20-25 Getting into the Mood/Warming-up

- Five-against-two on a marked-off section of the field, at first with as much ball contact as desired, then only two ball contacts followed by direct passing.
- Kicking the ball while running loosely.
- Running with increasing speed while kicking the ball.
- Kicking the ball ahead, sprinting after it, performing a move with it etc.
- Propelling the ball with the sole of the boot.
- Include feints and deceptions.

30-35 Physical Condition

- The players jog loosely with the ball around the square.
- The players then perform hops and sideways-dashes.
- The whole team is then divided up into four groups. Each team stands at a corner-flag and, one after the other, the team-members sprint once around the field with the ball.
- The teams stand at the corner-flags as above. This time the whole team sprints around the field with the ball.
- All the players start running around the field simultaneously until one player has caught up with the player in front of him (a game of chase).

35-40 Winding Down

A game of competitive soccer follows and the training session is completed with a ten-minute jog around the field.

TIPS FOR THE COACH

The players warm-up by practising relaxed passing.

Each player should have a ball

Every player should have a ball. The square should be 20 m x 30 m.

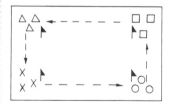

The coach should plan switches between individual and group competitions. The necessary pauses should be active.

Aims: Improving tactical playing and teamwork

A5

20-25 Getting into the Mood/Warming-up

- The players practise running with the ball.
- As above, but the players play the ball in a figure of eight between their legs.
- The players hold the ball between their legs with one hand in front of their body and one behind it. By changing hands quickly they try to keep the ball in the air.
- The players hop over the ball while it is lying on the ground.
- The players jump over the ball on one leg while it is lying on the ground.
- The players practise on their own with the ball and try out newly acquired skills.

30-35 Teamwork

- The members of a group of seven players pass the ball to each other.
- Each team divides up and plays three-against-four. The smaller team concentrates on practising dribbling, tackling and double passes. The larger team practises direct passing and passing with limited ball contact.

35-40 Winding Down

The players play a soccer game using two goals with extra points for goals scored by dribbling and double passes. Finally everybody jogs around the field for ten minutes.

TIPS FOR THE COACH

Each player should have a ball.

Loosening-up and stretching exercises should be built into these activities with the ball.

The players form groups of seven.

At first the teams play without goals: this can come later.

A6

Aime: Improving physical fitness using the ball

20-25 Getting into the Mood/Warming-up

Each player trains on his own with the ball, practising all the exercises learned to date. All this is carried out at a relaxed jog.

30-35 Techniques Course with Physical Exercises

1st exercise: Running with the ball through a slalom course.

2nd exercise: Finding a through ball.

3rd exercise: Juggling the ball.

4th exercise: Running with the ball, feinting all the time.

5th exercise: Goal-kicking from from various positions on the penalty line. This course is set up on one half of the field. On the other half, the rest of the team plays a game of soccer using mini-goals. The players form three teams. Two play soccer and the third goes through the course. Every team performs every activity at least three times.

30-35 Winding Down

Finally the team plays a soccer game using the whole field, placing emphasis on through balls. Lastly, everyone jogs around the field for ten minutes.

TIPS FOR THE COACH

One ball per player.

Each exercise takes about one minute to perform using full concentration.

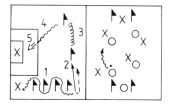

Aims: Improving tactical playing

20-25 Getting into the Mood/Warming-up
Individual practice with the ball:
- Running with the ball using the right, then the left foot.
- Juggling the ball.
- Practising feints, changes of direction and constant speed changes.

34-40 Tactical Playing
The players play in teams of three-against five, four-against-six, four-against-seven or five-against-eight
- The teams play from base line to the base line.
- Small goals are used.
- Instead of using goals, each team uses neutral kickers. These change their positions on the base line all the time, in order to receive the ball.
- The smaller team lures the larger team into going offside.
- The smaller team initially dribbles the ball then kicks it off.
- The larger team prefers to move around a lot more on the field and kicking double passes and direct passes.

25-30 Winding Down
In a soccer game using the whole the players practise of direct passing and offside positions. A ten-minute jog concludes the training session.

TIPS FOR THE COACH
Each player should have a ball.

The emphasis in this exercise is on the smaller team beating the larger team.

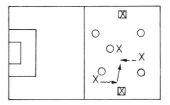

In case of tactical errors, the game should be halted and the player in question should be spoken to. The players should be made aware of alternative tactics.

A8

Aims: Improving endurance for Soccer

20-25 Getting into the Mood/Warming-up
- The players perform various relaxed passing moves within the group including loosening-up exercises.
- The players go through exercises in running with and juggling the ball.

30-40 Endurance for Soccer
The players form three teams of equal strength.
- Team A plays Team B using small goals. The size of the field should measure about 30 m x 40 m.
- Team C remains in the other half of the field, practising with the ball.
- Team A then plays Team C while Team B practises with the ball.
- Team B then plays Team C while Team A practises with the ball. If the teams are capable, these exercises can be repeated.

20-25 Winding Down
Each player jogs with the ball around for 20-25 minutes, performing various exercises.

TIPS FOR THE COACH
The players form three groups, each group with a ball.

Three teams.

The game should last about 5-8 minutes.

Each player is given a ball.

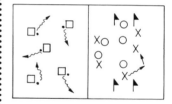

Aims: Training in goal-kicking

A9

20-25 Getting into the Mood/Warming-up

Each player practises by himself with the ball and should concentrate on those techniques he feels need improvement.

30-35 Goal-kicking

- Each player dribbles the ball from the centre line towards the goal and kicks a goal.
- At the centre line players start dribbling the ball towards a lead player standing at the 16-metre line who bounces it and then kicks it into the goal.
- During the above exercise a further player can be put on defence to stop goal-kicks.
- The first player dribbles the ball as above, but kicks a double pass to the lead player. These two players then play one-against-one as attacker and defender before one player attempts to kick a goal. The defending player is thus partly involved at first (with the double pass), then fully active on defence.

35-40 Winding Down

Four teams play a tournament. Each team plays the other for 5-8 minutes.

A versus B   C versus D
A versus C   B versus D
A versus D   B versus C

Everybody jogs for about ten minutes before leaving the field.

TIPS FOR THE COACH

Each player should have a ball.

Several groups of players kick goals into two or three goals so that the waiting period is as short as possible.

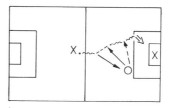

A10

Aims: Improving physical condition using the ball

20-25 Getting into the Mood/Warming-up

Pairs practise various passing moves receiving the ball; hitting the ball; keeping the ball in the air; practise feints with role-changes.

30-35 Exercises with the medicine ball

The players form two groups. While the first group carries out exercises with the medicine ball, the second group practises goal-kicking using two small goals. The groups alternate between activities several times medicine ball exercises:

- Practising throwing-in the ball all over the field.
- "Rowdy Rugby": two team-members play one-against-one and try to gain possession of the ball from one another from one 16 m-line to the other one. (see p. 68).
- One player throws the medicine ball between his legs backwards to his partner.
- One partner throws the medicine ball to his partner in mid-jump.
- Each partner throws the medicine ball to his partner alternatively with the right and left hand.
- One partner catches the medicine ball on in mid-jump and throws it in mid-jump back to his partner.
- The partners throw the medicine ball to one another while jogging slowly.

35-40 Winding Down

A game of soccer using the whole field, followed by a ten-minute jog around the field, completes the training session.

TIPS FOR THE COACH

The players form pairs with a ball for each pair.

The groups alternate between activities. Every round can be repeated several times. Each exercise should contain an "exertion" time of about 30-45 seconds with a corresponding rest period. One round with the medicine ball should last no more than ten minutes.

Aims: Improving general endurance
         Improving teamwork

A11

20-25 Getting into the Mood/Warming-up

Each group of three players practises passing the ball emphasising the following points:

- Double passes.
- Kicking the ball hard from a distance.
- Dribbling, with feints.
- Calling for the ball by sprinting.

30-35 Endurance Training and Teamwork

- Teams A and B play against each other on one half of the playing field trying to kick the ball into two small goals.
- On the other half of the field Team C goes through an endurance course.

After ten minutes the teams change places and Team B plays Team C emphasising the following points:

- Double passes.
- As little ball contact as possible.
- Counter-attacking.
- Moving the game all over the field.

35-40 Winding Down

The team plays a game of soccer using the whole of the field, paying attention to the above points of emphasis.

Before jogging off the field, every player practises by himself with the ball.

TIPS FOR THE COACH

The whole team divides into three groups.

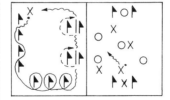

A12

Aims: Improving dexterity and agility with the ball

20-25 Getting into the Mood/Warming-up

The players juggle the ball in various ways:

- With the instep.
- With the thigh.
- With the head.
- The above moves should be carried out standing still and while moving;
- With flints.
- While dribbling the ball.

30-35 Dexterity and Agility

- The players run round in small circles with the ball, guiding it with the inner and outer edges of the foot at an ever-increasing speed.
- The players run with the ball from one side of the field to the other and change their relative position on the field.
- The players run with the ball through a narrow lane of other "disrupter" players.
- As above, except the lane contains players who try to intercept the ball.
- The players practise close running with the ball in a labyrinth marked by triangles.
- The players dribble the ball on a restricted field (10 m x 10 m) trying simultaneously to take the ball from other players and to keep one's own ball.

35-40 Winding Down

In a five-against-three game, the larger team has to pass the ball directly. In a four-against-four game or a five-against-five game, four goals are used, tournament-style. Finally the players jog for 8-10 minutes before leaving the field.

TIPS FOR THE COACH

Every player should have a ball.

Efforts should be made to evade the oncoming player. This means taking one's eyes off the ball. When running with the ball, movements should be close and quick.

The stress period should last about 30-40 seconds, followed by a relaxed trot. Positions should be changes several times.

3.4   15 Indoor Training Units

H1

Aims: Improving general dexterity with the ball
Improving co-ordination and agility

10-15 Getting into the Mood/Warming-up

- "Fire, Water, Lightning": all the players run around the gymnasium. When the coach calls one of these words, the players follow the above commands set out at right as quickly as possible.
- „The Chain-Gang" (See p. 22.).

TIPS FOR THE COACH

"Fire" = lying on one's stomach on the floor; "Water" = having no contact with the floor and looking for a piece of gym-equipment. "Lightning" = the players huddle together in the corner of the gym.

25-30 Dexterity with the Ball

The players bounce the ball on the spot as follows:
- With the left hand.
- With the right hand.
- Around the body.
- High and low.
- Through the legs.

The players bounce the ball while moving as follows:
- Everybody runs higgledy-piggledy over the gym bouncing the ball.
- The players bounce the ball with their right and left hand respectively.
- The players bounce the ball, sit down and stand up again.
- Clapping hands between each bounce.
- Doing a complete 360° turn.
- Doing a forward roll.

The players bounce the ball while running around the gym and try to knock out other players' balls.

Each player should have a ball.

The players should take their eyes off the ball to avoid colliding with other players.

This exercise can be performed as a competition with points.

25-30 Winding Down

The players play a tournament in teams of three-against-three with a goalkeeper. To finish off everyone runs slowly along all the lines on the floor of the gym.

Depending on the size of the hall more players can be used.

Aims: Getting used to the ball and improving the feel for the ball
         Learning agility and dexterity

H2

10-15 Getting into the Mood/Warming-up

The players dribble the ball:
- All over the playing field.
- At the sound of the whistle they stop immediately.
- Dribble the ball in a circle.
- At the sound of the whistle sit on the ball.
- Dribble along the lines painted on the floor.
- Perform a forward roll while dribbling the ball.

Exercises with the medicine ball: all players stand at the front of a volleyball court with a medicine ball in the middle. Each team tries to move it by kicking a football at it.

25-30 Getting Used to the Ball

- Collecting soccer balls: in the middle of the gym is a crate of balls. One or two players keep emptying the crate, the others collect the balls and put them back in the crate.
- "Copycat Dribbling": the coach dribbles the ball and all the players imitate his movements.
- The players play a dribbling-relay up to and around a turning mark.

25-30 Winding Down

Finally the "Little Guys" play a tournament against the "Big Guys" – this is determined by physical size. Everybody then slowly runs ten laps of the gym.

TIPS FOR THE COACH

Every player should have a ball.

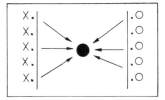

The object is to see whether a team can empty a crate. Playing time is about 30-60 seconds. The teams then change places.

H3

Aims: Improving the feel for the ball
Teaching co-ordination, agility and dexterity

10-15 Getting into the Mood/Warming-up

Various obstacles are set up in the gym (small crates etc). The players dribble the ball.

- The players dribble the ball around the obstacles, using the right and left foot alternatively.
- The players lift the ball over the obstacles, run around them and regain control of the ball. This exercise can be also be performed with both feet.
- The players lift the ball up in front of the obstacle, throw it up into the air and head it over the obstacle.
- The players use the obstacles as a wall for double passes.

25-30 Getting a Feel for the Ball

- This exercise starts with a dribbling relay.
- This is followed by a slalom-dribbling relay.
- Keeping the field clear. The gym is divided into two sections by two benches. Two teams stand opposite each other. Each player should have a ball. At the sound of the whistle, each player throws his ball onto the other side. Each team has to keep its half of the court clear of balls, which can be thrown or kicked.

20-25 Winding Down

A game of soccer follows, using two handball goals. Finally all players jog slowly around the court for about five minutes before leaving.

TIPS FOR THE COACH

Each player requires a ball

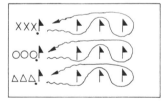

The object is to see which side has the least balls on its half of the court after 1-2 minutes. This game can also be played with soft balls.

Aims: Improving ball techniques

H4

10-15 Getting into the Mood/Warming-up

Each player performs a dribbling/ goal kicking relay: dribbling the ball in a slalom around triangles, performing forward rolls on the mat; running after the ball and finishing with a goal-kick. He then catches the rebounding ball cleanly and dribbles it back to the start. This exercise is performed without a goalkeeper.

25-30 Improving Ball Technique

- Several long benches are set up side-by-side in the gym. Each player then dribbles the ball along beside them and then performs a double pass.
- The player then dribbles the ball past the benches, performs a double pass at the end and finishes up with a goal-kick.
- These exercises can also be performed using the wall of the gym, providing it has no equipment standing or leaning against it.

20-25 Winding Down

For the final game, four goals are marked with flags, two on each side. The teams then plays a small tournament. While jogging off the court, the players have to run through each goal ten times, taking care not to run through any one goal twice in succession.

TIPS FOR THE COACH

The players form groups of 5-6.

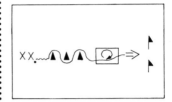

This can be performed with two goals.

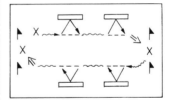

H5

Aims: Improving the feel for the ball

10-15 Getting into the Mood/Warming-up

"Day and Night": two teams stand on the centre line, two metres apart. At the call "Day" or "Night" the team called to has to catch the other. The players can start from various positions:

- Lying on their stomachs.
- Lying on their backs.
- From the "push-up"-position.
- Sitting back-to-back.
- Standing on one leg.
- From a squatting position.

25-30 Getting a Feel for the Ball

"Four-Goal Soccer": soccer with four goals. A substitute player waits behind every goal. This player is brought on every time a goal is scored and the goal scorer then waits behind the goal.

20-25 Winding Down

"Mat Soccer": several mats are placed all around the sides of the gym. Every team has to defend several mats, and they may score goals. The object is to see which team can score the most goals.

While jogging around before leaving the gym, each player has to touch each mat ten times, but these must always be on opposite sides of the gym.

TIPS FOR THE COACH

Players can only be caught out inside the the playing area. Make sure there is enough room for the players to run around in.

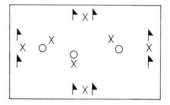

Alternatively the goals can be marked by flags, triangles or even players standing with their legs apart.

Aims: Improving the feel for the ball

H6

15-20 Getting into the Mood/Warming-up

The players dribble the ball:
- With the right foot, then the left.
- With the inside, then the outside of the foot.
- The players throw the ball gently up into the air and catch it.
- The players throw the ball up into the air, perform a forward roll and catch the ball properly, even if it has hit the floor first.

25-30 Ball Control, Catching and Running with the Ball

- The players dribble the ball to the front end of the gym, kick it against the wall, turn around and dribble it to the other side of the gym and so on.
- The players try to kick the ball continually against the wall at floor-level and at waist-level.
- The players throw the ball up against the wall and catch it cleanly on the rebound.
- "Wall Relay": the first player kicks the ball against the wall and the second player does the same. After having his turn, each player goes to the back of the line.

25-30 Winding Down

This time a soccer tournament is played on a mini-field. Each team plays against all the others. Before leaving the field each player has to run as many laps of the gym as goals were scored in the last game.

TIPS FOR THE COACH

Every player should have a ball. The players should try to avoid colliding with each other.

If not enough walls are available, flat surfaces of various sports equipment can be used instead.

During these exercises attention should be payed to the use of both feet.
The object is to do this 5-10 times without a mistake.

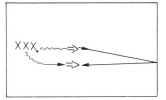

H7

Aim: Improving ball heading techniques

15-20   Getting into the Mood/Warming-up

- "Mat Relay": the players form groups of 5-7 members. Each group has two mats. Each group has to cover a given distance by moving the mats. The players are not allowed to touch the floor while doing this.
- "Catch": the mats lie all over the gym floor and count as "free" areas, where players may not be caught out.

25-30   Games Involving Heading the Ball

- "Shadow-Dribbling": one player with the ball dribbles the ball and his partner jogs behind. They then change places. Alternatively, the ball may be bounced with the hand.
- One player throws the ball in an arc to his partner who heads it back in the same manner.
- Partner A throws the ball up into the air and heads it into the goal. His partner then does the same and so on.
- Large tyres hang in every goal. Each player throws the ball up into the air and heads the ball through the tyre.
- Three players form a trio, consisting of a goalkeeper, ball-thrower and ball-header. The ball-header stands in front of the goal and heads back the ball which the other player throws to him from the side.

25-30   Winding Down

The team plays handball using two goals. Goals may only be scored by heading the ball. The players then head the ball in a dive on the floor-mat.

TIPS FOR THE COACH

Two players have one ball between them.

The goals stand opposite each other about 5 m apart.

Flying dives on the soft floor-mat are very popular and are good practice for heading the ball in a dive.

Aims: Improving basic technical skills

H8

15-20 Getting onto the Mood/Warming-up

- The players dribble the ball with the right then the left foot.
- They throw it up into the air and catch it again.
- They stop the ball with the sole of their boot while dribbling it and then continue dribbling.
- They juggle the ball.
- They throw the ball against the wall of the gym and stop it on the rebound with their chests.

25-30 Circuit Exercises for Soccer

The round can be completed several times without a break:

1st exercise: Dribbling the ball in a slalom course

2nd exercise: Juggling the ball.

3rd exercise: Throwing the ball against the wall of the gym and catching it again.

4th exercise: Goal-kicking.

5th exercise: Making a double pass at the wall or an up-ended bench.

6th exercise: Dribbling.

7th exercise: Throwing the ball into the air, heading it and catching it.

8th exercise: Throwing the ball against the wall and stopping it with the chest.

After each round, there is a one-minute class in ball practice before the next round starts.

25-30 Winding Down

The team plays a soccer tournament with teams consisting of only a few players. The defending players play against those on the offensive. After each game the players run three laps of the field.

TIPS FOR THE COACH

Each player should have a ball.

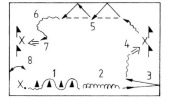

H9

Aims: Training in techniques for exercise rounds

15-20 Getting into the Mood/Warming-up

The players run various forms of "accordeon"-races:

- Running onto the field.
- As a one-against-one race.
- As a rally-race.

25-30 Practising Playing Techniques Using Circuit-training

1st *stage:* Slalom-dribbling.

2nd *stage:* Juggling the ball.

3rd *stage:* Lifting the ball with the foot and catching it cleanly.

4th *stage:* Kicking the ball continually against the wall.

5th *stage:* The goalkeeper keeps throwing the ball to the player, who then heads it into the goal.

6th *stage:* Each player heads the ball against the wall as often as possible without stopping.

If a player completes the course, he may have a break which he spends dribbling the ball.

25-30 Winding Down

Games using beer mats: The players form two teams and, at a sign from the coach, each team gathers as many beer mats as possible. As an alternative, one team lays beer mats on the floor with the coat of arms facing upwards, the other team places them with the other side facing upwards. The object is to see how many beer mats each team has when the final whistle blows. Finally the players jog off the court running between the beer mats lying on the floor.

TIPS FOR THE COACH

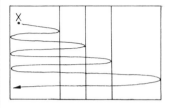

The exercises at each stage last about three minutes. More than one player can practise at each point at the same time.

Another variation is to have four teams playing this game seated in each corner of the gym.

Aims: Improving general fitness

H10

15-20 Getting into the Mood/Warming-up

The players practise on their own with the ball, practising the techniques they have learned and trying to invent new ones.

25-30 Improving Physical Condition Using Circuit-training

Five or more players can practise at each of the following practise stages:

1st stage: The players slowly run five laps of the gym. They are only allowed to sprint along one side.

2nd stage: The players perform skipping exercises using both feet, then the right foot, then the left.

3rd stage: The players lie on their backs with their legs apart and throw a medicine ball against the wall of the gym.

4th stage: The players throw the medicine ball while lying on their stomachs.

5th stage: The players then jump backwards and forwards over a small crate.

This process can be repeated several times.

25-30 Winding Down

The players perform the following exercises with balloons:

- Keeping a balloon in the air with various parts of the body.
- Jamming a balloon between their legs and running around with it.
- The players compete to be the first to touch all the yellow balloons lying on the ground etc.
- Two players jam a balloon between their bodies and try to take it to the finishing line.

TIPS FOR THE COACH

Each player should have a ball.

Each activity lasts 30-45 seconds. The players then take an active break of 30-45 second using a ball.

Hands, elbows, knees, nose, heels etc.

This game can also be played as a relay.

H11

Aims: Improving speed

15-20 Getting into the Mood/Warming-up

The players perform the following exercises:
- They jog 4-6 lengths of the gym.
- Stretching exercises.
- Strengthening exercises e.g. push-ups.
- Exercises designed to increase speed e.g. short sprints.
- Sideways gallops, hop, skip and jump, kicking the ball with the heel, hopping on one leg, hopping etc.

30-35 Speed Training

- Chasing an opponent around two or more long benches: several benches are placed end-to-end in the centre of the gym, around which the players run. The players form two teams for this purpose.
- Members of one team, then the other, sprint one after the other once around the two benches.
- Each team completes 2-3 laps.
- Team-pursuit: each team starts at opposite ends of the two benches. When any one team is the first to reach the other end, the race is over.
- Each team sprints, then jogs a lap around the gym and so on.

35-40 Winding Down

Finally the teams play a soccer tournament. Each team should have 3-4 members. If smaller teams are formed, the tournament can be played across the width of the gym. The players should not forget to run several laps before leaving the gym.

TIPS FOR THE COACH

Warm-up exercises without the ball.

Depending on the size of the gym this part of the training session can be tried with and without the ball. The players' technical skills should be taken into consideration here.

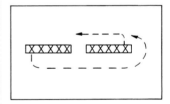

In order to maintain competitive spirit, the exercises should be selected in a manner that permits the players to take the necessary breaks. Speed training is not speed endurance training.

Team-size is determined by the size of the gym.

Aims: Improving general physical fitness with a partner

H12

20-25 Getting into the Mood/Warming-up

Easy jogging and various exercises:

- Passing the ball with the inner and outer side of the foot.
- Shadow-running.
- Dribbling the ball on a one-against-one basis with an active opponent.
- Stretching exercises are worked in.
- Juggling the ball, keeping the ball up in the air.

30-35 Improving Physical Fitness:
Exercises with a Partner

- Push-up competition: both players perform push-ups face-to-face and try to clap hands with each other.
- Both partners sit back-to-back with arms entwined. Each player tries to force his partner onto the ground on one side or the other.
- Pulling competition: each player tries to pull his partner over a line on the floor of the gym.
- Each player carries his partner piggy-back.
- Wrestling: one player lies on his stomach and his partner has to force him onto his back. The players then change places.
- Sprint-race or a chase around a long bench.
- The players see who can do the chin-ups.

35-40 Winding Down

The players form small teams and play soccer tennis. They then run a few laps of the gym to finish off the training session.

TIPS FOR THE COACH

Every two players are given a ball.

These exercises are carried out with a partner and contribute to improved physical fitness by playing games. The exercises can be performed one after the other or all at the same time by various players and can be carried out as exercise rounds with units lasting 30-45 seconds each. An active pause is required after every seven exercises.

H13

Aims: Improving playing-techniques in groups

20-25 Getting into the Mood/Warming-up

Each group has a ball and performs the following exercises:
- Warm-ups with various forms of passing.
- Mini-games of five-against-one or four-against-two.
- Keeping the ball in the air with the head, feet or thighs.

TIPS FOR THE COACH

The players form groups of 4-6 players.

30-35 Improving Techniques in Groups

- Continuous passing in a part of the field of a given size while on the run.
- Passing the ball while running towards a partner.
- Zig-zag passing of the ball from a standing position to other team-members standing in two rows.
- Group-juggling of the ball: various forms of passing: Player A dribbles the ball towards the goal, followed by Player B. With the sole of his boot Player A pushes the ball backwards to Player B, who kicks it into goal.
- Various forms of passing with a final goal-kick.

Each exercise should last about 4-6 minutes.

35-40 Winding Down

The team plays soccer tennis in tournament form. It then jogs around the court before leaving the gym.

The team practises the techniques it has just learned.

Aims: Improving playing techniques
in game situations

H14

15-20 Getting into the Mood/Warming-up
- "Catch 10" played as handball: two two groups of six members play each other. Each group tries to have the ball passed to it without being touched by the opposing team.
- "Tag" played without the ball: Player No. 1 catches Player No. 2, who catches Player No. 3 etc
- "Tag" without the ball: Player No. 1 catches Player No. 2. The other players have a rest. Player No. 2 then catches Player No. 3 etc etc.

30-35 Improving Playing Techniques in Game Situations
- "Handball-headball" using a goal.
- Dribbling slalom relay ending in a goal-kick.
- Four-against-two or five-against-one soccer with a small field.
- Sprint race with the ball.
- Juggling the ball.

35-40 Winding Down
This begins with a soccer game with teams of unequal size. The sides are changed regularly. This is is followed by a soccer game with sides of equal size. The session ends with a jog around the gym.

TIPS FOR THE COACH
The team forms groups of six players. Every group is given a ball.

The time spent at each stage is about 4-6 minutes. After every second stop, the players take a break by light jogging.

At stages 4 and 5 the group is divided into two teams of three players each. At half-time the teams change positions.

H15

Aims: Improving general physical fitness

20-25 Getting into the Mood/Warming-up
Various relay-races with and without the ball.

30-35 Improving Physical Condition
- Hurdle-relay: on the way to the turning point the following hurdles have to be surmounted:
  - A sprint to the first mat followed by a forward roll.
  - Jumping over the vaulting horse with legs apart.
  - Jumping over a long bench with five squat turns.
  - Hopping around the mat on one leg.
  - Then a sprint to the turning point and back.
- Ball-relay:
  - Juggling balls over the mats.
  - Ten direct passes against the bench;
  - Dribbling through a triangular slalom-course.
  - Throwing the ball against the wall five times and catching it.
- Relays with the medicine ball:
  - Sprinting to the mat, putting the medicine ball down and jumping over it five times.
  - Jamming the medicine ball between the legs, jerking it up into the air and catching it five times.
  - Throwing the medicine ball at a certain point on the wall five times and catching it again.

35-40 Winding Down
Small groups of players play "Tussleball" (see explanation p. 68) with the medicine ball. The session ends with a jog around the gym.

TIPS FOR THE COACH
Each group has 4-6 players.

3.5 Special Training for Individual Team Positions

S1   Special Training for the Goalkeeper

Goalkeeper Training

Special training for the position of the goalkeeper involves making very different demands at various stages of development of children and teenagers.

Phase 1 (Children Aged up to 10 Years)

Observations show that it is players in this age-group who are not suited – for whatever reason – to be field-players, who guard the goal. But the game and the various exercises available at this stage are quite varied and are designed to serve as a general form of basic training. For this reason it seems to make good sense for every player to have a turn as goalkeeper. This goes for training as well as league matches.

For this reason all children must not only be made familiar with foot techniques as part of a general ball training but also with the goalkeeping techniques. The following exercises are therefore designed to be completed by all team-members: catching the ball, fending off the ball with the fists, diving after the ball, rolling properly when falling, hitting the ball out of one's hands, running out and fending off the ball with the feet, taking up the proper position in standard situations (corner-ball, free kicks).

Phase 2 (Ages 10-14)

Towards the end of the first phase the real goalkeeper will have emerged and begins a specialised form of training for his specialised task.

As the teenager reaches his optimal learning-age in the prepubescent stage (ages 10-12), good learning points present themselves. These manifest themselves in the following exercises:
-   A well-developed sense of anticipation, being able to see in advance where the ball is going, being able to predict the movements of members of his own side and those of the opposing side.
-   The growth in the size of the body muscles.
-   A well-proportioned body.
-   Much improved physical co-ordination.
-   Speed and improved reaction as a result of increased muscle co-ordination – trainable suppleness and agility.

The object at this stage must be the development and improvement of the above-mentioned goalkeeping techniques in their basic form.

During puberty (ages 12-14) the body begins to increase in height and movements become uncoordinated. In this period of weakness and instability the teenager must be kept interested in the task of a goalkeeper and the training for this position is now directed at consolidating his previously acquired techniques. But the emphasis should be on manoeuvrability and agility. If the training is properly designed, the teenager can retain his basic motor patterns.

Phase 3 (Ages 14-18)

The teenager now enters his second learning period and his body proportions gradually approach those of an adult. The goalkeeper's technical and tactical performance must be further improved and refined.

He must learn self-control in standard situations, be able to catch the ball properly, fend it off with one or both fists, run out at the right moment, block the ball with his feet, direct the members of his team in front of him, predict the moves of the opposing side, try out defence moves by individual opposing players, set up his wall of defensive players properly, develop strategies against goal-kicks from the 11-metre line and much more. At the same time it is important that he succeeds in developing his own individual style.

On the Playing Field

Getting into the Mood/Warming Up

Each goalkeeper should have a ball in order to:
* Bounce the ball while running around.
* Throw the ball lightly up into the air and catching it while standing still or while running.
* Throw the ball up into the air and catching it while jumping or running.
* Throw the ball forwards diagonally or into the air and then catching it.

Practice-Phase

The following exercises should be carried out with a partner.
* Both goalkeepers throw the ball to one another and catch it (at chest-height, slightly to the right and to the left, above the head and from a hard bounce).
* Both goalkeepers play the ball to each other with a drop-kick.
* The goalkeeper stands on the 5 metre line. Another player then throws the ball up into the rear corner of the goal.
* The goalkeeper stands with his legs apart about 7 m – 8 m in front of the goal. The coach passes the ball through the goalkeeper's legs, who turns 180° and tries to catch hold of the ball by diving after it.
* The goalkeeper throws the ball over his head straight up into the air and dives after a second ball thrown to him by the coach. The goalkeeper then quickly jumps up to catch the first ball before it hits the ground.
* The goalkeeper stands in a goal marked by flags. One player stands in front of the goal, another behind, thus providing a challenge for the goalkeeper on each side. This requires the goalkeeper to be able to turn quickly.

The goalkeeper stands in the goal. Between 5-6 players practise in the penalty-area. The goalkeeper alters his positional play according to the demands of the game.
* The situation is the same as in the previous exercise, except that this time, the players also try to kick the ball into the goal.
* The goalkeeper stands in the goal. In front of it stand three players, who unhindered, convert passes intercepted from the outside.
* Following on from the above exercise two defence players are now also present.
* More passes are made in front of the goal and are converted by attacking players. Meanwhile other players kick goals directly from the penalty-line and a series of cross-kicks on the right, goal-kicks from the penalty-area, cross-kicks from the left etc then develops.

- A few players dribble the ball towards the goal and try to dribble it around the goalkeeper, who hurries out to defend the goal.

Tips for the Coach

- All training in goal-kicking is training for the goalkeeper at the same time.
- The goalkeeper must be basically put under competitive pressure.
- Almost every goalkeeper has a weaker side. This must be taken into greater consideration during goalkeeper training.
- The goalkeeper's performance from the point of view of physical fitness and techniques can be improved in individual exercises e.g. by training in takeoff-power, diving and catching, positional playing, hitting the ball out of the hand, long-distance throwing etc.

In the Gymnasium

The following exercises can be particularly important training for goalkeepers:

- Two goalkeepers throw a medicine ball to each other while jogging slowly.

- Two goalkeepers throw a medicine ball to each other in an arc and catch it while jumping up into the air.

- One goalkeeper throws the ball up into the air and both keepers then jump after it in an attempt to catch it.

- Falling practice onto a soft mat:
    - Throwing the ball left and right. The goalkeeper tries to catch it.
    - A player throws the football to the left and to the right into the goal. The goalkeeper tries to catch it from a squatting position.
    - The goalkeeper does a forward roll and then tries to catch the ball as it is thrown to him.

- The soft mat lies on the floor by the wall. The goalkeeper stands on it, about 3 m from the wall with his back to it:
    - His partner throws the ball against the wall. The goalkeeper turns around quickly and has to catch the ball on the rebound.
    - The goalkeeper stands with his face to the wall and has to catch the ball when it is thrown.

S2   Special Training for Defending Players at Right and Left Wing

• A midfielder kicks the ball towards one of the attacking wingers, who is covered by one of the defending players. The latter tries to gain possession of the ball. If he succeeds, he kicks the ball back to the midfielder.

• A defence player shadows a winger, who tries to shake off the winger by suddenly accelerating. The midfielder then passes the ball.

• The midfielder passes the ball to the winger again. The defence player tries to gain possession of the ball. The player with the ball pursues his course to the goal area and finally attempts a goal-kick.

• The midfielder passes the ball to the attacking winger and the defending winger tries to gain possession of the ball. If he does not succeed, the attacking winger runs towards the goal, but is then attacked by the roving defence player. The attacking winger can now pass the ball to the midfielder who has run with him or dribble it himself. He then kicks the ball at the goal.

• The midfielder kicks the ball up into the air to the attacking winger, so that the latter has to receive it with his head. The defending winger tries to intercept the ball with his head.

Besides safe defensive play and good positional playing with ball and opponents, the ability to attack is also expected from an attacking winger. That means that he must immediately switch from fighting to gain possession of the ball to a counter-attack. This can be learned using a small goal set up on the centre line.

S3   Special Training for the Roving Player

The roving player is usually the free unattached behind the defence. He is the last resort if the defence in front of him has been breached. He therefore requires special positional playing abilities as well as the ability to range over the playing field unhindered. He frequently leads the attack when the team is on the offensive. These features of his ability determine the tasks for special training:

• The roving player stands in the defence area and receives the long kicks from mid-fielder A.

• The roving player stands in the defence area and receives the ball thrown by the mid-fielder as a head-catch.

• The roving player stands in the defence area, catches long-distance passes from the mid-fielder and goes immediately into the offence by kicking the ball directly to the other midfielders.

• A goalkeeper, a defence player, the roving player, an offence player and a midfielder play into the goal-area. The offence player and midfielders work together to outplay the defending player, and the roving player tries to attack the breached offensive by skillful positional playing.

• The goalkeeper, roving player, two attacking players, two defending players and a mid-fielder who passes the ball all play towards one goal. The roving player replaces any eliminated defensive players.

• The above tactics can be used by three attacking players against three defending players.

• Alternatively, this can be played on an uneven basis with the attacking players outnumbering the defence. In this case the roving player has to keep the field covered.

• Two teams play against each other using two goals. If the roving player or a defence player intercepts the ball, they can counter-attack immediately.

S4 Special Training for the Midfielder

The midfielders play both on defence and offence. They reinforce the defence and help form the offensive. Their duties range from preventing the other side from scoring goals to kicking goals.

- Several players move freely around a cordoned-off area of the field. The midfielder kicks the ball to them and gets it back in the form of a pass. The kick-off takes place while on the run or in the open area of the field.

- The midfielder only comes in contact with the ball twice between every kick-off.

- The midfielder passes the ball on immediately.

- The midfielder now makes long-distance passes instead of the short-distance passes he has made in the past.

- A defence player now joins the players to whom the ball will be passed. As soon as a player breaks away, the midfielder passes the ball to him.

- A player on the offensive has to break away in order for the midfielder to pass him the ball without giving the defending player a chance to intercept.

- This game between the three players is now concluded with a goal-kick.

- Other variations of this game are: two-against-two plus the midfielder or three-against-three with the midfielder. Either way the players should attempt to kick goals.

The midfielder should bear in mind the following points when attacking:
- He has to make passes directly to the front.
- He has to kick the ball out of the back row.
- He has to make double-passes with the players on the offensive.
- He has to move the game around on the field.

S5   Special Training for the Attacking Wing Players

In today's normal playing it is no longer possible to talk about "just a winger". By constantly rotating the players, individual positions are also continuously changed and therefore reference is usually made to "spearheads". Nevertheless the qualities of the winger are also still very important these days. For this reason special training for the striker is generally a good idea. But the players on defence or the midfielders are also in this position sometimes.

- The player quickly dribbles the ball along the sideline towards the base-line and kicks the ball diagonally at the goal.

- As above, but this time the player has to outplay, i.e. get the ball past, a defending player.

- A midfielder kicks off, the striker takes over the ball, gets it past the defender and makes a pass in front of the goal.

- The striker goes past the defender on the inside and performs a goal-kick.

- The striker kicks a pass at the short corner and then at the long corner.

- The striker kicks a pass from a standing position and while running at full speed.

- The striker kicks a pass along the ground, at waist-level and into the air.

- The striker draws his flanks in directly from the sideline, if possible at the rear of the defence.

S6   Special Training for the Centre-Forward

The centre-forward develops a great push towards the goal. He tries this by kicking goals and by heading the ball. He must also be a good dribbler. Accordingly, these are also the requirements for special training.

- He must practise goal-kicks from all positions.

- He must practise goal-kicking after a player from the other team has been eliminated.

- He must kick a goal immediately after making a tackle.

- A midfielder kicks the ball to a centre-forward who is covered by a defending player. The cenre-forward then makes a back-pass to the midfielder.

- The midfielder kicks off again. The centre-forward shakes off the opposing defending player by a deception and kicks a goal.

- The players kick balls at waist-height to the centre-forward, who receives them, shakes off the opposing defending player by means of a deception and kicks them into goal.

- The ball is bounced high in front of the goal. The centre-forward then has to get it past the defending players in order to head it into the goal.

- The midfielder kicks the ball to the centre-forward, who bounces it back. The midfielder then passes it back to the centre-forward, who then attempts a goal-kick.

- The striker makes ground-level and high passes to the centre-forward in front of the goal. The centre-forward has to accept these and convert them into goal-kicks despite the efforts of the defending players.

3.6   Tips on Tactics

T1 Tactics

The development of an understanding of tactics is closely connected with a player's intellectual abilities. This is why the teaching of tactics must be oriented to the intellectual development of children and teenagers.

From ages 5 to 10 (Midgets, Junior E's and F's) the children are only capable of grasping the basic idea of the game, namely, "scoring goals and preventing the other side from doing the same". At this age the capacity for abstract thought is not sufficiently developed to put blackboard explanations of tactics into practice, for example. Using appropriate and easily-understandable game situations, trainers of children in this age-group must aim at developing a gradual and subconscious understanding of tactics. At this age, the children typically run in a tight group, each child trying simultaneously to gain individual possession of the ball.

Intellectual development and the capacity for abstract thought increase in the Junior D's (ages 12-14). The simple basics of tactics can now be taught and put into practice, such as the task of keeping to individual positions within the team. The positions of the star-players in the First Division of the Federal German Soccer League can be used as examples here.

Intellectual development in the Junior C's (ages 12-14) reaches its initial height for this purpose. All important fundamentals of tactics must be acquired here. Since many players have reached a certain level of technical ability, they can afford not to look at the ball so often while playing and concentrate on tactical knowledge and how to acquire it.

In the following years (Junior A's and B's) these developmental tendencies are built on and reinforced under competitive conditions.

T2   The Main Principles of Tactics

The following are a few important basic concepts and principles relevant to the development of an understanding of tactics.

Individual Tactics

How the individual player acts when in contact with an opposing player e.g. running around on the field, dribbling the ball, passing, positional playing, tackling, pushing and shoving, goal-kicking, blocking the ball etc.

Group Tactics

This involves cooperation with members of one's own team in countering the opposing team e.g. running around on the field, making double passes, giving up the ball to other team members or receiving it from them, playing on the wing, covering other players or sections of the field or luring the opposing team offside.

Team Tactics

These are measures adopted by the team as a group to counter an opposing team during a game e.g. strategy, countering-moves, playing for time etc.

Certain aspects of tactics can now be developed, depending on the ages of the players. This takes place among other things through the use of games with teams of uneven size.

T3   Various Ways to Counter a Strengthened Defence

* Kicking fron the second row.
* Frequent changes of position.
* Intensifying the game at the wings.
* Kicking the ball to the striker at the outside line.
* Dribbling and subsequent cross-passing.
* Double passes.
* Changing speed.
* Moving the game to other parts of the field.

T4 Teaching Counter-attacking

Counter-attacking from a strengthened defence is frequently used against stronger teams or in away-games. In order to mount a successful counter-attack, the following prerequisites are usually important:
* Fast offensive players who can also dribble well.
* The ability to call on the defensive players in the attack.
* The ability of the players to make long passes.

Here is an example of an exercise in counter-attacking:
* Variations of long passes in groups of two or three players.
* Games of six-against-six or seven-against-seven using a normal-sized goal with a goalkeeper. The defending team tries to gain possession of the ball and counter-attack by kicking the ball between two small goals marked by flags on the centre line.

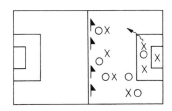

* As above but with a counter-attack using long diagonal passes.
* As above, but all players of the attacking team have to move up a row e.g out of the penalty area.
* As above, but with an additional "no-go" area in the middle of the playing field, so that the attacks have to be carried out over the wings.

T5 A Few General Principles

* When dribbling, the player should bring his body between the ball and the opponent.
* Always go to the man with the ball.
* Don't let the ball bounce.
* Go towards the ball.
* Shake off the opposing player when your own team gets or is in possession of the ball.
* Each player has to play even when he is not in possession of the ball.
* Support your fellow players by constantly offering to take over possession of the ball.

3.7   Areas of Special Emphasis for Coaching

Important Points and Planning-aids for Coaching in Fitness-training for Adolescents at Each Stage of Development

As mentioned earlier, the dividing of training into periods corresponding to the various stages of the players' physical and psychological development is of assistance to the coach.

The players develop continuously; which means that there are certain "grey areas" and transition points between the various phases respectively.

The available training must be correspondingly flexible.
The following points may be of additional assistance to coaches and practice coaches.
• The pre-pubescent stage
Maximum strength and strength endurance should only be increased under certain conditions. Increased speed, on the other hand, can be easily trained.
The aim in this phase is the strengthening of all important groups of muscles through the use of exercises in the form of games. Speed-training should certainly start here i.e. reaction, basic speed can be easily increased. Speed endurance, on the other hand, should not be taught (because of reduced non-respiratory capacity).
Children in this stage of development can be easily trained in endurance (using games for the respiratory area). This is also the best age for learning motor skills.
During this period, all important techniques should be made available in a form suitable for children. At this age (7-10), co-ordination skills also reach their peak (the age of dexterity).
• The first stage of puberty
Maximum strength, endurance and speed are easy to train. Because of unfavourable leverage abilty i.e. increase in height, this gain appears at first glance to be negligible.
At this stage the potential for the improvement in respiratory endurance is good. ("If the changes in the heart-lung area are not sufficiently tested at this stage, the biological endurance stress potential in adulthood will not be attained" – cf "Fußballpraxis, 3. Teil, Jugendtraining I"). These omissions cannot be made up for later. (Non-respiratory endurance training must, of course, be foregone!).
The ability to learn motor skills decreases markedly and the learning of new skills is made more difficult. The training emphasis is therefore on reinforcing those rudiments of the game already familiar to the player.
• The second stage of puberty
Maximum strength and elasticity can now be learned (e.g. improved lever-ability of the joints). The emphasis is now on strength endurance training. Training for endurance of the respiratory system also has its place here.
Techniques are refined, made automatic and are consolidated through the stress of competition. Co-ordination training now proves more successful again.

Z1   Endurance Training in Childhood (Junior E to C Teams)

The players are gradually and methodically introduced in stages to a slow and sustained running pace.

- **"Run and Guess!"**
  The players try running for 1-2 minutes without the ball. Those that think that the time is up, sit down. The object is to see who has the best feeling for time. This exercise is repeated several times with varying time periods e.g. 30 seconds, 90 seconds, 3 minutes. Variation: as above, but two players run together and pass the ball to each other. The same exercise can also be carried out in groups of three.

- **Keeping the Same Speed**
  A large running track is marked out on the playing field. The players have to run one lap of the field within 20 or 30 or 40 seconds. After 10, 15, or 20 seconds, the coach blows his whistle, by which time the players must have completed half the course. If the players are too fast or slow, they adjust their times in the second half accordingly.

- **Running Laps**
  A large running track is marked on the field or in the gym out as above. The players run five or ten laps. The coach then stops his stop watch and the players run the same number of laps as before in the opposite direction and try to complete them within the same time.

- **Biathlon**
  Everybody is familiar with the combination of downhill skiing and shooting. Here, however, there is a slight alteration. The players run several laps around the field or gym and then have to kick the ball at a target such as a tenpin, a small goal or a medicine ball. The players should try to hit the target at least three out of five times. If a player does not reach this minimum, he is required to run a penalty lap.

- **Interval Running**
  The coach jogs a given distance with the players based on their ability. The course is regularly interrupted by breaks in which the players carry out gymnastic exercises with a ball. The players then continue running until the next break.

- **"Run and Guess"**
  After the players have developed a sense of time, the following "Run and Guess" game can be played. The players know the exact length of the course to be run. Each player

tries to say as accurately as possible how long it will take him to complete the course. The object is to see who can come as close as possible to that time.

- **Guessing Shapes**
  The first player in a group runs to a certain shape on the ground e.g. in the shape of a house, and the other group-members have to guess what the shape is. However the other players may only have one guess. The player who guesses correctly is allowed to take over the position of the first player and run a new shape for the other to guess.

These and other opportunities for running may be carried out on the playing field, in the gymnasium or on an open piece of ground. The running may be accompanied as far as possible by exercises with a ball, whether related to soccer or not.

Stretching

Indispensible for warming-up and Winding Down

Stretching exercises are part of every warm-up programme. The choice of a few exercises selected according to how relevant they will be to the point to be emphasised during training later, is especially useful.

Every player carefully feels towards the edges of his personal limits and stretches his body according to what he feels is right for a period of 10-20 seconds.

Demanding training-exercises are followed by gymnastic relaxing-exercises, so that the muscles retain their elasticity and performance.

The following basic programme is designed for the most important groups of muscles that are used when playing soccer:
- Warm-up first e.g. with easy jogging and running.
- Breathe calmly and regularly while stretching. Never hold your breath.
- Select stretching exercises for the most important muscles used during a soccer game: shoulder, chest, hips, back, stomach, thighs, calves and ankles.
- Practise by yourselves and do not compare your performance to that of anyone else on the team. Stretching is not a competition; rather, it is individual work for your own bodies.
- Carry out the exercises correctly, otherwise their effect will be lost.
- Take up the positions shown in the following illustrations without any jerky movements (no bouncing) and maintain them for up to 20 seconds. Then loosen up and relax.

No. 1: Stretching the thigh muscles:
- Stand with your legs apart.
- Your trunk should be upright.
- Transfer the weight of your body to the bent legs.

No. 2: Stretching the adductors:
- Bend the upper part of your body forward.

No. 3: The rear muscles of the lower leg:
- Press your heels onto the ground.
- Transfer the weight of your body forward and
- Support your body on the wall using your hands.

No. 4: The thigh muscles:
- Keep your bodies upright.
- Ensure your back does not form a "hollow".
- Press one foot against your buttocks.
- Push your pelvis forward.

No. 5: Shoulder, upper arm and chest muscles:
- Position your bodies at right-angles to the wall.
- Lay your arms on the wall behind.
- Stretch your body by turning it away from the wall.

No. 6: The rear thigh muscles:
- Bend your body forwards at right-angles to your legs.
- Stretch your knees out.

No. 7: Stretching the inner trunk muscles:
- Draw your heads between your knees from a semi-crouching position.

No. 8: The back, shoulder and chest muscles:
- Stretch your knees.
- Bend the upper part of your body in a horizontal position until your back is traight.

No. 9: The side muscles of the trunk:
- Push your hips sideways.
- Push your trunk in the opposite direction.
- Lean the upper part of your body slowly sideways.

No. 10: The side trunk muscles:
- Adopt a standing position.
- Lift your arms over your heads.
- When leaning to the left, your left leg should be stretched forward and when leaning to the right, your right leg should be stretched forward.

No. 11: The back and leg muscles:
- Bend over and try to put your head through your legs. In the process, your knees will stretch.
- Draw your arms downwards, thereby reinforcing the stretching.

No. 12: The shoulder and arm muscles:
- Hold one arm behind your head.
- Press your elbow downwards with the other hand.

Z 2   Improving Physical Fitness

Circuit-training for Speed

- *1st Stage:*
  The players each sprint about 10-15 m. They then jog for a further 30 m. They then continue sprinting again etc.

- *2nd stage:*
  The players sprint through a 10-15 m-long zig-zag or slalom-course. They then jog for about 30 m.

- *3rd stage:*
  The players first sprint 10 m straight ahead, then 10 m backwards, followed by a 30 m-jog.

These stages can be repeated up to five times. Between each repetition the players take a break or a complete rest.

Requirements for Speed Training

- Distances of between 10 m and 30 m.
- Maximum speed.
- A 60-100-second break after each run (complete breaks).
- 4-7 runs (series).
- 2-3 series.
- 5-minute rest-periods between each series.

If the breaks or rest-periods are too short, training in speed endurance rather than speed should be emphasised.

Z 3   Improving Physical Fitness

Circuit-training for Endurance

- *1st stage:*
  The players hop 15-25 times in a forward and a sideways direction over a medicine ball or over a similar object (strengthening of the leg muscles).

- *2nd stage:*
  Each player throws the medicine ball 15-25 times to his partner as though he were throwing it in (strengthening of the arms and/or stomach muscles).

- *3rd stage:*
  Lying on their stomachs the players raise the upper part of their bodies 15-20 times (strengthening of the back muscles).

- *4th stage:*
  Lying on their backs the players raise the upper part of their bodies by bending their legs   15-20 times (strengthening of the stomach muscles).

- *5th stage:*
  The players perform 50-80 jumps with a skipping rope.

The above repetition times are for general guidance only.
The slalom/zig-zag course can be extended with further exercises such as hopping on one leg, push-ups and exercises with a partner.

Z 4   Improving Physical Fitness

Circuit-training for Take-off Power

- *1st stage:*
  The players hop over a row of medicine balls lying in a straight line on the ground.

- *2nd stage:*
  A player throws the ball to his partner, who jumps up and heads it back.

- *3rd stage:*
  Several barriers are set up on a running track for the players to jump over.

- *4th stage:*
  The players have to jump 50-80 times over a skipping rope, using the right and left foot alternatively.

- *5th stage:*
  The players jump along on the right, then the left leg alternatively for up to several metres. The leg in use must be drawn up to the body after the leap has been commenced.

These exercises can be repeated 5-10 times, but it must be remembered that the stress and rest-periods should last about 30 seconds.

Criteria for Speed Endurance Training and Take-off Power Training

- Jumping: 5-10 consecutive jumps.
- Height and distance of jumps: as high and as far as possible.
- Speed: as fast as possible.
- After a series of jumps: 60-100 seconds break.
- Number of jumps in a series: 4-6.
- Number of series: 2-3.
- Complete rests between series: approximately 4-5 minutes.

Z 5   Combined Fitness Training (Strength and Endurance)

General Fitness Training and its Application in the Game

The players form two groups. Group A carries out a round of circuit-training and Group B takes part in a programme of running activities or plays a game of soccer using two small goals.

After ten minutes, each group switches activities. Several series of activities may be carried out.

The circuit-round contains stress phases and rest phases lasting about 30 seconds. The circuit consists of the following activities:
- Push-ups.
- Sit-ups with the legs bent.
- Throwing a medicine ball from either a kneeing or a sitting position and then catching it from a standing position.
- Either hopping or jumping on one leg over a hurdle-course consisting of medicine balls placed about 50-60 cm apart.
- Lying on their stomachs, the players straighten their bodies and throw a ball from their left hand to the right hand and back again.
- Jogging for 4-5 minutes.

Speed
- Speed training is a 3-5 second burst of exertion with active breaks consisting of relaxed jogging lasting 1-2 minutes.
- The breaks must be so designed that the body can recover completely i.e. with a pulse-rate of under 120.
- "Anaerobic Training should not begin until ages 17-18 and even at this age, there must be as little training as possible to increase on speed endurance." (AUSTE, N.: Konditions-training Fußball, Hamburg-Reinbek, 1987, p. 48).

Forms of training designed to increase in speed are:
- Various starting positions, "Day and Night", "Catch in a Circle", games of catch, relays, dribbling-relays, etc.
- Sprints of between 10-30 m in length with breaks of 90-120 seconds in length.
- Running at ever-increasing speeds.
- Exercises to increase co-ordination.
- Games with only one or two instances of contact with the ball.

Strength Training

Strength Training has various forms
- Maximum strength training, consisting of weight-lifting with only three repetitions at the most (pyramid training).
- Speed-training: 6-8 repetitions carried out as rapidly as possible, with complete rest-periods.
- Strength endurance: this time medium exertion is required, with only 20-30 repetitions. The   breaks do not permit a complete recovery before continuing.

Training designed to increase strength includes:
- Jumping, hurdling, jumping in a restricted area (nimbleness).
- Games and exercises with the medicine ball on one's own and with a partner.
- Exercises with a partner. Competitions between partners e.g. cossack-dancing, cockfighting, wrestling.

Endurance

Following are a few tips for the conducting of endurance training:
- Choose a running speed that permits the players to enjoy themselves (average running speed).
- Training should last between 10-30 minutes.
- The pulse rate shoud be about 130-160 beats per minute.

Training designed to increase endurance includes:
- Seeing who can run for 10-15 minutes without stopping.
- Games in small groups (five-against-five or eight-against-eight).
- Running in squares or triangles (Junior A's and B's)
- Long-distance running interspersed with gymnastic exercises.
- Hurdling.
- A six-day run.
- One-against-one dribbling (using two small goals) lasting 80-90 seconds.

The following are criticisms about Speed Endurance Training:
- Excessively high stress stimuli leading to concentrations of lactates far above the normal competition levels. As a result, training is not ideally adjusted to the stress of competition.
- Increased production of lactates e.g. high acid levels, leads to reduced training economy and thus to reduced training effectiveness, so that performance stagnates or is even reduced. (The performance of the central nervous system is affected, causing

general fatigue and reduced concentration, and technical performance is ruined over the course of several hours.)

- The increased effect of training on the muscle cells and hence, an increase in performance in the sense of supercompensation, is not possible; in fact, performance decreases the effectiveness of the muscle cells.
- Repeated speed-training during the week leads to reduced endurance and a decrease in acceleration when starting to run. In other words, it achieves the opposite effect.
- Training for anaerobic endurance must be reduced and discontinued in favour of speed when starting to run and while running (c.f. G. GERISCH/H. J. TRITSCHOKS: Schnelligkeitsausdauer. In: Fußballtraining No. 2/83, p. 15 f.).

"In the area of school-, youth-, and trainee soccer it is particularly important – if at all – to give speed endurance training in small doses and not to make too much of it, especially since teenagers' and young adults' vegetative nervous systems have low resistance to large stress loads, resulting in the exertion of unnecessary training.

From a physiological point of view, there is no plausible reason for soccer players in this age-group to carry out special speed enduranc training." (H. LIESEN: Schnelligkeitsausdauertraining im Fußball aus sportmedicinischer Sicht In: Fußballtraining, No. 5/83, p. 27 f.).

4 A Check-list for the Planning of a Soccer Tournament

The junior sections of many soccer clubs plan tournaments over the course of a year. Such events can take place outside on a normal-sized field or a smaller field for junior players as well as in the form of an indoor tournament in winter.

Tournaments of this sort can take on an "international" character through the participation of teams from other countries.

As such school- and youth-tournaments are already a tradition in many clubs and thus have set or fixed dates, it is a good idea to discuss these (dates) with any newcomers to the club. When planning, preparing for and carrying out such tournaments, there are many points to be considered. These are listed below.

4.1 Planning

Before an invitation to a tournament can be extended, there are numerous preliminary points to be considered, and the leader of the club's youth section should discuss these with the youth committee. The club's management committee is then informed of the result of these deliberations. Points for consideration are:

- Setting a date: weekend, public holidays, or some other time when there are no league matches taking place.
- Approximate length: from when till when.
- Place: triple-hall gymnasium buildung (indoor tournament). Junior-sized or normal-sized field (open-air tournament). Number of available gymnasiums and soccer fields.
- Number of participants: four, six, eight or 16 teams are ideal.
- Guest teams: should the invitations go to teams from the same country or from overseas? How can their addresses be obtained?
- The number of players and replacements, and their ages.
- Accommodation and catering; ascertaining the cost of these outgoings.
- Drawing up an estimated budget of the cost of the whole event.

4.2 Preparation

If the proposed youth tournament has received the approval of the club's junior section and executive committee, and if planning has been successfully completed, the preparations can begin:

- The establishing of an organising-committee – which may consist of all those responsible for the club's youth section – and the issuing of tasks to the responsible committee-members.

- The producing of an announcement of the tournament with information on venue, date, who is eligible to participate (determined by the age of the players), the size of the teams, form of tournament, length of each game and the rules, timetable for the game, accommodation, catering, costs, prizes, registration formalities and registration forms.
- Reserving the playing fields and/or gymnasiums respectively.
- Obtaining approval for the tournament from the responsible Regional or National Soccer Committee.
- Requesting the necessary referees.
- Sending out the invitations and announcements of the tournament to the teams selected for participation, giving the last date for reply.
- Final arrangements for accommodation and catering for all teams; final confirmation of participants after all clubs have replied.
- Arranging social events for the guest teams: civic reception, sight-seeing, tours of the city, entertainment evening, religious worship etc.
- Finding a patron for the tournament.
- Formation of an honorary committee made up of prominent personalities who could also be approached for a donation.
- Finding sponsors from commerce and industry.
- Donation of trophies by prominent personalities from the world of politics, sport, business, art etc.
- Appointment of people to escort the guest teams during their stay.
- Drawing up a script für all those involved in organising the tournament, giving all necessary information concerning: time, activity, task, who is responsible.
- Arranging any necessary transport for the teams.
- Appointment of those to take charge of correspondence, accommodation, catering and transport, financial matters, team escorts, the referees and the organising of the social events.
- Obtaining commercial quotes for food and beverages on the playing fields or in the gymnasium.
- Sending invitations to guests-of-honour, club-members and other visitors.
- Supplying information to the media (daily newspapers, free neighbourhood newsletters, local radio and TV stations) before and after the event.
- The donating of a "Fair Play" prize.
- Obtaining practice- and competition balls.
- Appointing of linesmen.
- Arranging for alternative venues in case of inclement weather.

4.3   Going ahead with the Tournament

If the preparations have been carried out properly, the tournament should go well, but even during the tournament there are many tasks to be performed:

- Greeting the guest-teams on arrival and getting them to their accommodation.
- A meeting of all team escorts to discuss all sporting matters before the start of the tournament.
- The formation of a three- or five-member steering committee responsible for the settling of disputes during the tournament.
- The official opening of the tournament with greetings, opening addresses, music and perhaps a brief sporting event.
- A social evening with entertainment to break the ice between hosts and guests.
- The completion of the tournament with a ceremony for the winners, presentation of trophies the farewelling of all the teams.

4.4   The De-briefing

Finally, a de-briefing is held to record the positive points of the tournament. Problems must also be addressed and solutions found for the future, but the de-briefing is not a time for looking at the efforts of individual organisers and helpers in a critical light.

- All those in charge should each make a list of what went well and not-so-well in his area of responsibility.
- Using their lists, they then meet and discuss all these points. Problems are discussed and new solutions found.
- Using the suggested changes, the tournament script is added to and corrected as required for the next tournament.

5   The Social Side of Junior Soccer

As everybody knows, soccer is a team-game and for this reason, good relations between the children and teenagers are an essential part of youth work. Anyone responsible for young people who is only capable of teaching training and competitive games, will in the long run, not be able to retain the young people as club-members.

A club must be able to offer young people more than just sport. Besides the specialist area of "soccer", it must be able to offer a replacement for lacking sense of community experience. As long as children and teenagers feel comfortable in a sports club, they will seek direct contact with it.

Hence the following suggestions for activities and events that the team can take part in as a group. These, of course, must be adapted to local conditions. Age and social structure of the club's youth section or team, and the preparedness of those in charge to get involved in such activities, also have an influence.

If we can develop a "us"-feeling in the youth section or team, the experiences of the boys and girls as a group will lead to greater harmony in the sporting sector.
    Solid teamwork, specially adapted for young people, thus becomes one way of promoting increased sporting performance.

One of the marks of a good sports club is the leisure activities it offers off the sports field. It must appeal to young people in such a way that identification with the team is desirable.

5.1   Social Events

Social events are an opportunity for having a long pause. They break up everyday life and are fixed points that people aim at. There are many reasons for a party. Here are a few:
- The team has a sports-related reason for celebrating e.g. promotion to a higher league, a championship win, the first win in a round, managing to avoid being down-graded into an lower league, tournament victory etc.
- One of the players, coaches or helpers has a birthday.
- The team is invited by a youth-section manager, parents, club sponsors or some other patron to a party.
- A new player, coach or youth-manager joins the team and celebrates his first day with the team. The departure of somebody from the team can also be an opportunity for a party in order to wish that person well.
- A coming festival might also be an occasion for a party e.g. club anniversary, Christmas, the beginning or end of the of the soccer season, the summer holidays etc.

These are only some of the reasons for having a party, but it should be mentioned at this point that the children and teenagers should be involved in the preparatory activities.

We would like to mention the following activities which might also serve as occasions for social events:

- The team should work out the most original ritual possible for celebrating every birthday. It should discuss how to expresses its best wishes to the person concerned, who in turn should consider how he or she will express his or her thanks.
- A player, coach or manager may have had an interesting overseas holiday and could show scenes in slide films or on video.
- A film evening could feature a new training film, videos of the latest world championship or a movie of some description.
- The junior players could organise a disco in the local childrens' home and could choose the records/CD's or even the disc jockey themselves. Another group could present a short comedy stage act or a sports event during the interval.
- The whole team could go on a trip to a national or regional soccer championship match or, if the opportunity presents itself, even a championship event in a totally different sport.
- The team could organise a soccer tournament, with a programme like that of a real tournament.
- The team could organise a table tennis tournament with invited guests. Assistance may be required from any local table tennis club. Singles and doubles can be held, with the doubles teams being chosen by lot.
- In winter a badminton-tournament could be organised in the gym. Assistance could be sought from any badminton fans in the club or from any local badminton club.
- During the winter break the team can go ice-skating at the local ice-skating rink – provided there is one. Leather gloves should be worn.
- A rally on foot through the town or forest can be great fun when the whole youth section is divided into groups according to teams or when the whole team is divided into pairs. Each group then has to perform certain tasks.
- The team could get together for a barbecue at a barbecue site in the woods or on the club premises. Everybody can bring something, depending on what is needed. Who brings what can be decided beforehand (charcoal, food, drinks, etc.).
- "Let's play Father Christmas or the Christ Child, but without dressing up!" In the period leading up to Christmas the team could think about doing something for less fortunate children or teenagers e.g. inviting a group from the local childrens' home, giving them presents and involving them in an afternoon of games etc.
- The team can, of course, also go to the theatre. For the very young members, this might consist of a performance of fairy-tales or childrens' tales.

The older teenage members may prefer musicals or light comedies. Regional or   dialect theatre is also very entertaining.

- Interesting visits e.g to an artist's studio, a newspaper or to a weather station or weather observatory are also conceivable.
- Perhaps an author of childrens' or teenagers' stories might agree to come and read some of his or her own works.
- Many towns and cities have historic buildings or institutions. One can learn a lot about one's home town or region from a knowledgeable guide who knows how to make such topics interesting for young people.
- Many towns organise fairs over the course of the year. A visit to such a fair can do a lot to reinforce team spirit.
- The team can spend an afternoon or evening at the local childrens' home with the theme "Board Games Preferred". Team members can bring board games from home and can teach others the rules.
- In rural areas the team might be able to find a forest ranger or hunter who would agree to take the members out one night or early one morning to observe the local wildlife.
- If there are (older) skiers in the team, they could perhaps be prevailed upon to organise a winter ski-trip to the mountains or to a cross-country ski area. The list of suggestions can be added to as desired. However, it is important for youth leaders to find out what is available in the local area in respect of sporting, social and cultural interest.

5.2   Team Trips

Each team or its junior section undertakes trips of one or more day's duration.

These may be carried out in connection with sporting events or simply in order to reinforce team spirit. These excursions should be combined and extended with various other activities.

- A visit to an animal park.
- A visit to an open-air museum.
- A boat-ride on a lake, dammed-up lake or river.
- A visit to an adventure park.
- For the very brave, a raft-ride or canoe-ride.
- Helping out in a farm-yard or with the harvest.
- Camping out in tents including sitting around a camp-fire at night.
- A pony-ride through a forest.
- A ride in a covered wagon (western-style).
- For the teenage members, a visit to a factory might be interesting.
- A guided tour around an airport or aerodrome.
- A visit to a television studio (including the sports section) or film studio.
- A visit to a min.

- A stay at a sports training school in preparation for the coming season or to bridge the gap during the winter season.

The number of such visits can be added to as required, but it always depends on what is available locally. Those options that are of special interest for young people and in which they can take an active part are preferable.

5.3   International Matches

For soccer teams in those areas bordering other countries, international matches are already an everyday event. However, most other teams require a little peparation for unfamiliar overseas situations.

Therefore it is important to take some of the pressure off the "overseas novices".

The following tips may help to make an overseas trip a little easier:

- The team's ability to communicate in a foreign language may be limited and team-members may need to make themselves understood in sign-language occasionally. Young people are frequently able to communicate in English.
- In the country being visited, the inhabitants have different customs. The team must remember and respect this, and behave accordingly.
- The cuisine is also different from that at home. If dishes and beverages which are un-familiar or known at home by a different name are offered, then it sometimes behooves guests to respect these differences.
- Before leaving, the trip leader should make sure that everybody has adequate medical insurance, including provision for medical evacuation.
- The youth leader arranging the trip and accompanying the team should obtain any necessary information on the host country beforehand. This can be obtained from some-one who knows the country in question, who comes from there or who has travelled there frequently. Alternatively, travel guides containing all necessary information can be obtained from a bookshop.
- Passports or other internationally recognised travel documents are required for all over-seas trips. As children and teenagers sometimes do not always possess such documents, these must be applied for well in advance. The issue or extension of such documents can sometimes take a long time. Before departure the trip leader should check that everyone has a passport or other travel document with him and that it is still valid. Lost travel documents can be replaced with the assistance of the visitors' Embassy, High Commission, Consulate-General or Consulate.
- Some countries may require visitors to obtain visas. The trip leader should ascertain whether this is the case or not and ensure that these are applied for in sufficient time.
- In some cases the host country may have special regulations concerning the import of local or foreign currencies e.g. the amount, declaration upon entry/departure etc. These points should also be checked.

- When children or teenagers are out on their own in a foreign country, they should carry their accommodation address or a meeting place with them in order to ask passers-by the way back to the team.
- Before the trip the group-members should find out about the legal tender of their country of destination and the exchange-rate. A talk on souvenir-buying may help to avoid overspending.
- With sporting and private contacts, giving a small gift or club pin can be a very kind gesture. Each player should also prepare a number of hand-written address cards to take with him or her for any future correspondence.
- The trip leader should also make sure that any team-members with medical conditions e.g. asthma have enough appropriate medication with them as well as an official medical prescription for replacements (this includes those team-members who wear spectacles or contact lenses).
- If possible, names addresses and telephone numbers of medical practitioners in the area that the team will be travelling to and who speak the team's language should be obtained.

6 Further Reading

ALBECK, TH./ZÖLLNER, H.: Kindgerechtes Fußballtraining, Handbuch für Jugendtrainer und Sportler/innen, WFV-Schriftenreihe Bd. 27.

AUSTEN, N.: Konditionstraining Fußball, rororo Taschenbuch, Reinbeck bei Hamburg 1987.

BAUER, G.: Fußball perfekt: vom Anfänger zum Profi, München 1974.

BAUER, G.: Die aktuelle Situation des Jugendtrainings, Fußballtraining 8/9, S. 4-10 (1988).

BAUER, J.: Über die Bedeutung „sensibler Phasen" für das Kinder- und Jugendtraining, Leistungssport 4, S. 9-14 (1987).

BISANZ, G./GERISCH, G.: Fußball: Training, Technik, Taktik, Reinbek bei Hamburg 1988.

BISCHOPS, K./GERARDS, H. W.: Tips für Spiele mit dem Fußball, Meyer & Meyer Verlag, Aachen (1989).

BREMER, D.: Jugendfußball heute, Fußballtraining 8/9, S. 31-36 (1988).

BRÜGGEMANN, D.: Kinder- und Jugendtraining, Schondorf 1989.

DEUTSCHER FUßBALL-BUND: Fußball-Lehrplan 2: Kinder und Jugendtraining, Grundlagen, München 1985

DEUTSCHER FUßBALL-BUND: Fußball-Lehrplan 3: Jugendtraining, Aufbau und Leistungen, München 1987.

HAHN, E.: Kindertraining, Probleme, Trainingstheorie, Praxis und Sportwissen, München/Wien/Zürich 1882.

HAMSEN, G./DANIEL, J.: Fußball Jugendtraining, herausgegeben von B. Gottwald, Sport rororo, Rowohlt verlag, 1990.

HOLLMANN, W. U. A.: ZUr kardio-pulmonalen Trainierbarkeit unter besonderer Berücksichtigung der präpuberalen Phase, leistungssport 1, S. 11-15 (1983).

MARTIN, D.: Training im Kindes- und Jugendalter, Band II, Verlag Hans Huber.

PFEIFER, W./MAIER, W.: Fußball, Jugendtraining II, 4. Teil, Technik, Taktik, Kondition, WFV.Schriftenreihe Nr. 20.

WITTMANN, F./MAIER, W./PFEIFER, W.: Fußball-Praxis, Jugendtraining I, 3. Teil, Leistungsbestimmende Grundlagen, Mannschaftsführung, WFV-Schriftenreihe, Bd. 15.

ZINTL, F.: Ausdauertraining, Grundlagen, Methoden, Trainingssteuerung, blv-Sportwissen, München/Wien/Zürich 1988.

LEISTUNGSSPORT: Zeitschrift für die Fortbildung von Trainern, Übungsleitern und Sportlehrern, herausgegeben vom Deutschen Sportbund, erscheint zweimonatlich, Philippka-Verlag, Münster.

DER FUßBALLTRAINER: Fachzeitschrift für alle Trainings- und Wettkampffragen, Achalm-Verlag, Reutlingen.

FUßBALLTRAINING: Zeitschrift für Trainer, Sportlehrer und Schiedsrichter, herausgegeben von G. Bisanz, Philippka-Verlag, Münster.

Soccer Training

Klaus Bischops/
Heinz-Willi Gerards
**Coaching Tips
for Children's Soccer**

Coaching Tips for Children's
Soccer is a complete guide for
ensuring that young players get
the most out of the game – psy-
chologically, socially and
physically. Starting with the belief
that fun and self discovery are
the most important aspects of
any sporting activity for children
up to the age of 10, the book
covers the basic principles of
child development and details
60 play-oriented training units.

128 pages,
10 photos, 3 figures
Paperback, 11.5 x 18 cm
ISBN 3-89124-529-7
£ 5.95 UK/$ 8.95 US/
$ 12.95 CDN/€ 9.90

Jürgen Buschmann/
Klaus Pabst/Hubertus Bussmann
Coordination
A new Approach
to Soccer Coaching

Modern soccer is distinguished
by perfect ball and body
control at top speed. For this
reason training in movement
and ball skills are becoming
more and more important.
Coordination skills are therefore
among those factors that
determine performance in
soccer. This book describes
numerous coordinative forms of
play and training and is for all
coaches and sports teachers in
schools and clubs.

120 pages
Two-colour print
Numerous illustrations
Paperback, 14.8 x 21 cm
ISBN 1-84126-063-0
£ 9.95 UK/$ 14.95 US/
$ 20.95 CDN/€ 14.90

MEYER & MEYER Verlag | Von-Coels-Straße 390 | D-52080 Aachen, Germany | Fax +49 (0)2 41-9 58 10-10

Soccer

Gerhard Frank
Creative Soccer Training

In 40 different points of emphasis in training the book describes technique, tactical and fitness training according to the game method. The aim of the book is playful structuring of training in order to return the focus of soccer to game creativity, imagination and improvisation. Furthermore, trainers are given important tips on proper warming up and warming down. An index helps readers to quickly locate the required points of emphasis in the context of the various training games.

128 pages
Two-colour print
82 figures
Paperback, 14.8 x 21 cm
ISBN 1-84126-015-0
£ 12.95 UK/$ 17.95 US/
$ 25.95 CDN/€ 14.90

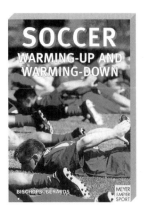

Klaus Bischops/
Heinz-Willi Gerards
Soccer – Warming-up and Warming-down

In this book the authors provide some 35 programmes for proper warming-up and warming-down for soccer. The programmes are full of variety to avoid monotony and are based around the game of soccer itself, within a team situation. The book proceeds from a basic understanding of the needs of every individual to stretch and ease their muscles and tendons, through a series of simple games and exercises using the football and other aids.

136 pages,
22 photos, 172 figures
Paperback, 14.8 x 21 cm
ISBN 1-84126-014-2
£ 8.95 UK/$ 14.95 US/
$ 20.95 CDN/€ 14.90

MEYER & MEYER Verlag | Von-Coels-Straße 390 | D-52080 Aachen, Germany | Fax +49(0)241-958 10-10

Training

Klaus Bischops/
Heinz-Willi Gerards
Soccer – One-on-One

Systematic and deliberate training in proper one-on-one behaviour is an indispensable element of modern soccer training. This book is designed to do justice to the great significance of the one-one-one situation in soccer. With competence and in great detail the authors describe everything you need to know about that specific situation.

160 pages
Two-colour print
21 photos, 88 figures
Paperback, 14.8 x 21 cm
ISBN 1-84126-013-4
£ 12.95 UK/$ 17.95 US/
$ 25.95 CDN/€ 14.90

Gerhard Frank
Soccer Training Programmes

Soccer Training Programmes contains a collection of 96 detailed plans designed to be used by amateur coaches. Each programme is based on knowledge and techniques developed in professional soccer and other sports which have been adapted to the specific conditions and needs of the amateur game. In clear and concise chapters "Soccer Training Programmes" also provides an overview of the key aspects of a coach's work, including physical training, skill development, tactics and psychological preparation.

216 pages
Numerous photos and figures
Paperback, 14.8 x 21 cm
ISBN 3-89124-556-4
£ 12.95 UK/$ 17.95 US/
$ 25.95 CDN/€ 16.90

MEYER & MEYER Verlag | Von-Coels-Straße 390 | D-52080 Aachen, Germany | Fax +49 (0)2 41 - 9 58 10 -10

Soccer Training

Erich Kollath
**Soccer –
Technique & Tactics**

The essence of soccer is really the interplay between technique and tactics. In modern soccer these two components must complement each other. The author first deals intensively with soccer technique, extensively covering all movements with, without and around the ball. In the second part tactics are discussed, whereby the author differentiates between the individual tactics of the various playing positions, group tactics and team tactics. More than 150 drills and game patterns provide a diverse range of ideas for learning and improving soccer technique & tactics.

152 pages,
83 photos, 28 illustrations
Paperback, 14.8 x 21 cm
ISBN 1-84126-016-9
£ 8.95 UK/$ 14.95 US/
$ 20.95 CDN/€ 14.90

Jozef Sneyers
**Soccer Training –
An Annual Programme**

This book offers soccer trainers over a thousand ideas and methods for the whole training year with their soccer team. Soccer expert Jozef Sneyers takes you from the pre-season period through the season itself to the following resting period. The flexibility coupled with an understanding of the structure of the complete annual programme make this book a useful companion to trainers for many years.

312 pages
Two-colour print
644 illustrations
Paperback, 14.8 x 21 cm
ISBN 1-84126-017-7
£ 14.95 UK/$ 19.95 US/
$ 29.95 CDN/€ 18.90

ME
&M
SP

MEYER & MEYER Verlag | Von-Coels-Straße 390 | D-52080 Aachen, Germany | Fax +49 (0)2 41-9 58 10-10